THE HIGHLY SENSITIVE PERSON'S GUIDE TO STOP PEOPLE-PLEASING

FINALLY, PUT YOURSELF FIRST, SET BOUNDARIES WITH CONFIDENCE, AND RELEASE THE NEGATIVITY IN SAYING NO!

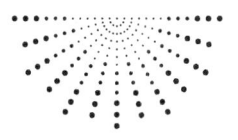

C. JEFFREY

Copyright © 2023 C. Jeffrey. All rights reserved.

The content contained within this book may not be reproduced, duplicated, or transmitted without direct written permission from the author or the publisher.

Under no circumstances will any blame or legal responsibility be held against the publisher, or author, for any damages, reparation, or monetary loss due to the information contained within this book, either directly or indirectly.

Legal Notice:

This book is copyright protected. It is only for personal use. You cannot amend, distribute, sell, use, quote, or paraphrase any part, or the content within this book, without the consent of the author or publisher.

Disclaimer Notice:

Please note the information contained within this document is for educational and entertainment purposes only. All effort has been executed to present accurate, up-to-date, reliable, and complete information. No warranties of any kind are declared or implied. Readers acknowledge that the author is not engaged in the rendering of legal, financial, medical, or professional advice. The content within this book has been derived from various sources. Please consult a licensed professional before attempting any techniques outlined in this book.

By reading this document, the reader agrees that under no circumstances is the author responsible for any losses, direct or indirect, that are incurred as a result of the use of the information contained within this document, including, but not limited to, errors, omissions, or inaccuracies.

CONTENTS

Introduction 9

CHAPTER 1 15
How Sensitive Are You? 15
There's sensitive, and then there's highly sensitive (Radhakrishnan, 2021) 16
Highly Sensitive Persons (HSP) (Scott) 17
The Four Main Characteristics of Highly Sensitive People (Snow) 20
Common Traits of an HSP (Scott) 21
How being an HSP can negatively impact your life (Snow) 24
A Highly Sensitive Person vs. an Empath (Orloff, 2019) 26
Introvert, HSP, or Empath? (Crosthwaite, 2020) 30

CHAPTER 2 33
Why You Are the Way You Are 33
Why do highly sensitive people feel everything so strongly? (Daniels, 2021) 35
Why do HSPs seem introverted, even if they're not? 40
Why do HSPs feel different or odd? 42
Why do HSPs struggle to say no? (Trittin, 2018) 44
Why is it hard for an HSP to speak up and ask for our needs to be met? (Sapala, 2018) 46

How the subconscious beliefs of an HSP affect our perception and interaction with others	50
Misconceptions about HSPs	54
CHAPTER 3	**59**
Please Stop Pleasing	**59**
Highly Sensitive People and People-Pleasing (Granneman, 2014)	60
How people-pleasing affects your relationships	65
Why people-pleasing is so dangerous for HSPs (Cerbo, 2016)	67
Why is it difficult to stop people-pleasing? (Mathews, 2015)	68
Breaking free from people-pleasing (Cherry)	72
Wrapping Up Chapter 3	81
CHAPTER 4	**83**
No Is Your Biggest Weapon	**83**
Saying no as an HSP (Granneman, 2014)	84
The importance of saying no (Prober, 2019)	86
How to say no as an HSP (Choby, 2020) (Prober, 2019)	89
How to say no without feeling guilty (Renzi, 2018)	96
Wrapping Up Chapter 4	100
CHAPTER 5	**103**
The Buck Stops Here	**103**
HSPs and Boundaries (Mackenzie-Smith, 2022)	104
How to start setting boundaries (Martin, 2021)	116
Putting your boundaries into place (Choby, 2020)	119

Enforcing your boundaries (Renzi, 2018)	124
Wrapping Up Chapter 5	127
CHAPTER 6	129
Creating Your Own Comfort Zone	129
Becoming aware of your emotions (Macejova, 2017)	130
Have a plan to protect yourself	134
Dealing with non-HSPs (Rose, 2020) (Bauder, 2021)	137
Advocate for yourself (Scott & Gans)	138
Create a 'Yes List'	140
Stress management tips and techniques (Scott) (Verghese)	148
Wrapping Up Chapter 6	150
CHAPTER 7	153
Embrace Your Highly Sensitive Self	153
The strengths of an HSP (Chloe, 2019)	154
Five ways to access your strengths (Snow, 2018)	161
The value you add to relationships as an HSP (Good Therapy, 2015)	164
How to harness your HSP qualities for your own good	167
Wrapping Up Chapter 7	171
BONUS CHAPTER	173
How to Deal with the HSP in Your Life	173
How to identify a highly sensitive person (Mind Tools Content Team)	174
How to support highly sensitive people (Mind Tools Content Team)	175
How to communicate with highly sensitive people	178
Why you need HSPs in your life	181

| *Conclusion* | 183 |
| *References* | 189 |

A FREE GIFT FOR ALL READERS!

STOP PEOPLE PLEASING
Meditation

SCAN THE QR CODE FOR ACCESS TO A MEDITATION THAT ACCOMPANIES THIS BOOK

INTRODUCTION

"When you say 'Yes' to others, make sure you are not saying 'No' to yourself."

— PAULO COELHO

"Why are you so sensitive?" "What's wrong with you?" "Don't be such a crybaby!" Do these sound like echoes from the past? Or maybe even now?

If you're anything like me, you've probably heard a lot of that, and it might have made you feel something is wrong with you—like you need to fix yourself. You might even feel you're the odd one out, and other people don't relate to how you think or feel. For years I was convinced I had a flaw that needed to be hidden and that I was doomed to live a second-rate life.

I was miserable, exhausted, and always overwhelmed, but I could never understand why or how to fix it. I dreaded social gatherings where I'd have to network and chit-chat with others. They always left me feeling fatigued with a deep desire to retreat to my own space. I hated that I always felt like I was absorbing everyone else's energy; it felt stuck to me and drained me. I felt I was always busy helping other people, and I never had time for any of my own dreams and goals, but somehow, I could not say *no* to people. I had this debilitating fear that they would reject me or start a fight with me if I didn't do what they were asking. I could never go to a movie with my friends without first vetting the movie for fear that it contained gore, violence or sad scenes that would make me cry. I felt like an outcast for so many years. I felt like there was something unfixable in me.

Quite the opposite is true, though. In fact, there is something very right with you and me, and I'm so glad I learned about it when I did because my life has completely changed for the better. Although it may feel like it at times, we are not alone—15% to 20% of the population is highly sensitive. You are not strange or weird; your brain merely functions differently. You are a highly sensitive person (HSP), which is a gift, even though it may not feel like it sometimes.

As someone who has struggled with high sensitivity my whole life, I understand what it feels like to be in your shoes. I understand the need to withdraw to a dark, quiet place after being around crowds of people. I know what it's like to feel anxious and overwhelmed by situations that don't seem to bother other people. I understand what it's like to feel sick when you witness violence, torture, or cruelty of any kind—even if it's in a movie. I used to be extremely negatively affected by criticism. I gave my time, effort, and compassion to others without receiving the same in return. And I would take responsibility for other people's happiness at my own expense. That is, until I discovered that my sensitivity is an innate trait and learned how to overcome its challenges. That is the journey I'm about to share with you.

This book is for you if you feel like you have no control over your sensitivity or your life. I am here to help you and guide you through a part of who you are that's been misunderstood by you and others for years. Together, we will work to overcome the struggles you face as a highly sensitive person so you can emerge on top and take back control—all while remaining true to who you are.

Here are a few topics we'll be covering:

1. **How sensitive are you?** Identifying if you're an HSP is the first step in taking control of the challenges you face because of your sensitivity.
2. **Why you are the way you are.** Understanding how the highly sensitive brain functions will clarify many things in your life and help you make peace with who you are.
3. **People-pleasing.** Highly sensitive people tend to people-please and make everyone else's problems their own. Acknowledging this characteristic and knowing how to break free is the next step on your journey.
4. **'No' is your biggest weapon.** Not saying *no* and people-pleasing are like two peas in a pod. When you learn to say no, you'll be able to confidently tell people that you can't help them without feeling guilty.
5. **Setting boundaries.** Establishing boundaries and learning how to implement them is one of the most essential parts of putting yourself first. Without proper boundaries, it is so easy for people to take advantage of your giving nature.
6. **Creating your own comfort zone.** As a highly sensitive person, it is very important to create a space that is a sanctuary for you to disappear to

when you're feeling overwhelmed. This isn't only a physical space but also an emotional one.
7. **Embracing your highly sensitive self.** This is the last step to taking back your life and your well-being. Once you realize that sensitivity is valuable and can be used for your own good, you will be unstoppable.
8. **How to deal with an HSP in your life.** It is important to help the people in your life understand how you function to be more aware of your needs and how they can be there to support you.

I wrote this book because I felt incredibly alone for so many years, and it wasn't until I stumbled on the topic of HSPs that I managed to embrace who I am and use my gifts to help the world. As someone trained in hypnotherapy, spiritual therapies, and trauma-informed care, I know how important it is to overcome anything holding you back, even if that means overcoming yourself. I put this guide together because I know full well that it's possible for an HSP to be sensitive and compassionate while doing what's best for themselves despite their innate tendencies.

This book will help you understand yourself and why you do the things you do. It will also provide strategies to help you address the difficulties of being an HSP and how to overcome them. My goal is to help as many people as possible embrace being highly sensitive and show them how to harness their power.

From one highly sensitive person to another, you deserve to love yourself and live a life of fulfillment and happiness—and it is completely possible. After working through this book, you will be able to step into the power of being a highly sensitive person and break away from the tendencies making you an easy target for manipulation.

CHAPTER ONE

HOW SENSITIVE ARE YOU?

Have you ever been told you should stop *overthinking* or are *too sensitive?* Do you feel that people who say things like that are insensitive? Don't you wish you could help them understand why you think and feel the way you do?

I can't stand chaos or loud environments. Bright lights hurt my eyes, and if I think someone was possibly a little rude in an email, I feel upset for the rest of the day (*cough* week). Being highly sensitive has both negative and positive traits. On the positive side, I am a very creative person, extremely connected to nature, and deeply spiritual. My sensitivity allows me to be a great support for those in need, and I can feel the positives in life more deeply. I am an avid appreciator of the small details in life that go unnoticed by most.

THERE'S SENSITIVE, AND THEN THERE'S HIGHLY SENSITIVE (RADHAKRISHNAN, 2021)

Sensitivity can be described as our response to the environment around us, either emotionally, physically, or spiritually. For example, sensitivity to pain or the cold means we have a lower threshold to that stimulus. The same thing happens with our emotions. Being a sensitive person doesn't only mean you're easily offended all the time. It also means you are caring, kind, aware of other people's needs, able to pick up on someone's feelings and behave in a way that makes others feel comfortable.

Being a sensitive person is a good trait to have. It helps us respond to our environment and the people around us. It also keeps us alert to danger. Sensitivity is the basis for empathy and feeling sympathy for someone else. Being sensitive aids in maintaining relationships, both personal and professional, and helps us with decision-making.

However, there is a difference between being a sensitive person and having overly heightened sensitivity. Being highly sensitive has its drawbacks and can affect our mental health, relationships, and work if not managed properly.

HIGHLY SENSITIVE PERSONS (HSP) (SCOTT)

Do you get teary-eyed when watching adverts for animal cruelty or illness? Are your feelings easily bruised, or do you constantly worry about upsetting others? Do you stay clear of violent and scary movies? Are you bothered by loud and irritating noises like sirens or music coming from someone else's earphones? If that's the case, you may be a highly sensitive person (HSP).

An HSP has an increased or deeper central nervous system sensitivity to emotional, physical, or social stimuli. This is often described as having sensory processing sensitivity (SPS).

These terms were first coined by psychologists Elaine and Arthur Aron in the mid-1990s. Although HSP is not a diagnosable condition, awareness of the concept has grown over the past few years. HSP is a trait that induces increased responsiveness to both positive and negative influences. However, being highly sensitive is far more than a personality type; it is a genetic trait.

Around 15% to 20% of the population are highly sensitive people. Unfortunately, that's too many for it to be classified as a disorder but not enough for it to be understood or validated by the majority of those around us. That really doesn't help our situation much, does it?

The HSP trait is innate, and biologists have found it in over one hundred species, including horses, cats, dogs, primates, birds, fish, and even fruit flies. The HSP trait reflects a specific type of survival strategy where one is observant before acting, meaning that the brain of an HSP actually functions a little differently from others.

Dr. Elaine and Arthur Aron conducted a study (McNamee, 2014) to investigate whether the traits of an HSP could be associated with identifiable genes, behaviors, physiological responses, and patterns of brain activity. They used a test called *functional magnetic resonance imaging* to examine the brain of eighteen married individuals. The participants were shown photographs of sad or smiling faces. The faces were a combination of strangers and the faces of their spouses. Drs. Aron found that the areas in the highly sensitive participants' brains associated with awareness and emotion showed a substantially greater blood flow than those with low sensitivity.

This is physical proof that HSPs respond especially strongly to social situations and stimuli that trigger emotions within the brain. The participants were scanned again a year later, and identical reactions were observed. According to the researchers, the results confirm that highly sensitive people are extremely tuned to their environment and that this emotional responsiveness and heightened awareness trait is inherent to this group of humans.

The HSP trait is not a new discovery, but it is misunderstood. Because HSPs prefer to observe and watch before entering a new situation, they are often labeled shy or unsociable. However, shyness is learned, not innate. Although this trait is repeatedly mislabeled as introversion, 30% of HSPs are extroverted. It has also been referred to as neuroticism, fearfulness, and being inhibited. Some highly sensitive people behave this way, but these traits are not instinctive either.

An HSP experiences life more intensely. They are more disturbed by tension, violence, and feelings of being overwhelmed. As a result, they make an effort to avoid situations where this would occur, such as large crowds, being around loud people, and even avoiding violent movies or TV shows. On the more positive side, HSPs communicate more efficiently because they don't only hear the words coming out of a person's mouth, but they also pick up on the most subtle changes in a person's tone or gesture. Increased sensitivity is also linked to higher levels of creativity, a greater appreciation for beauty, and richer personal relationships.

THE FOUR MAIN CHARACTERISTICS OF HIGHLY SENSITIVE PEOPLE (SNOW)

High sensitivity can show itself in many ways but generally shows up in four main characteristics consistent throughout the person's life, whether introverted or extroverted.

1. **Depth of processing.** The brain of an HSP has a more active *insula*, which is the part of the brain that increases self-awareness and enhances perception. An HSP is hardwired to pause and reflect before engaging in anything. HSPs are always absorbing a lot of information and thinking about it deeply. This can result in more transition time between certain tasks and slower decision-making.
2. **Overstimulation.** HSPs notice more subtle details in the environment around them and are more emotionally impacted by social stimuli. Because of this, their senses are more likely to be overstimulated, which can lead to exhaustion.

3. **Emotional Responsiveness/Empathy.** A scan shows that HSPs have more active mirror neurons, which are the parts of the brain responsible for feeling empathy toward others. HSPs also have more activity in the areas of the brain that are involved with emotional responses. HSPs feel emotions, both negative and positive, more intensely.
4. **Sensitive to Subtleties/Sensory Stimuli.** A person with HSP will notice subtle details that others overlook, like nonverbal cues and slight changes in their environment. HSPs are highly impacted by strong sensory stimuli like loud noises, bright lights, rough textures, and strong smells.

The remaining 80% of the population, which are not HSPs, do not possess all four of these characteristics or their associated implications.

COMMON TRAITS OF AN HSP (SCOTT)

Being highly sensitive has the advantages of loving, living, and feeling deeply, but it can also lead to feeling misunderstood, exhausted, and overstimulated.

Here are some common feelings experienced by an HSP, both positive and negative:

- Deeply moved by the beauty expressed in nature, art, the human spirit, or even a good commercial.
- A need for downtime, especially after a hectic day. HSPs don't just *prefer* downtime; they *need* it and feel like retreating to a dark, quiet room to recharge their batteries.
- Easily overwhelmed by physical and sensory stimuli like uncomfortable clothing, bright lights, and noisy crowds.
- Easily offended by people, even those who are being kind and mean no harm.
- A deep thinker who takes the time to think through every aspect of what has transpired before acting. This trait can cause slow decision-making.
- Avoids violent TV shows or movies because they leave you feeling uncomfortable and unsettled. Any form of violence is too intense.
- A deep, complex, rich personal life with deep thoughts and strong feelings to accompany them.
- Imagines different scenarios in which conflict could occur and avoids these scenarios altogether for fear of conflict happening.
- A heightened perception, intuition, and insight help you pick up on subtle emotions like

hostility and tension, which others may overlook.
- Detail-orientated and notices the minutiae that other people tend to miss.
- Feels the loss of a relationship deeply and spends time engaging in contemplation.
- Takes criticism harshly and personally and is easily offended.
- Emotionally reactive where your emotions highjack your behavior. You have knee-jerk reactions to your own feelings and strong responses to what others may be going through.
- Socially anxious and shy when around other people. You may prefer one-on-one interactions and meaningful connections.
- Experience guilt for saying no and worrying about hurting other people's feelings if you do. Setting boundaries is very uncomfortable for an HSP.
- Being misunderstood by friends and family leads to lower self-esteem.
- A deeper spiritual connection and love for nature and animals.
- Unfulfilled, burnt out, or overstimulated at work. You may find yourself changing careers often.

- Difficulty identifying your needs and being self-sacrificing leads to feelings of frustration, resentment, and anger.
- Tendency to be conscientious and honest leads to a commitment to doing things the right way.
- Being more caring and empathic toward others helps you tend to the needs of the people you love.
- Being an HSP means you're good at solving problems. HSPs are not "out of sight, out of mind" people and will keep working on a problem until it's solved.

HOW BEING AN HSP CAN NEGATIVELY IMPACT YOUR LIFE (SNOW)

Being an HSP has advantages and disadvantages. People with HSP tend to get more stressed out when faced with challenging situations. They may also find it tough to cope with scenarios that don't phase others.

Some of the ways that being an HSP can negatively impact your life include:

- You may feel overwhelmed and rattled when you have a lot to do in a short period of time, even if you do have enough time to get everything done.

- You are prone to being more stressed out by conflict and often misinterpret unrelated signals from someone as signs of anger or conflict.
- You are more stressed when faced with a difficult situation and are often more stressed by things other people don't have an issue with.
- Your intuition and empathy lead you to pick up on other people's needs and feelings. You hate letting people down and struggle to say no, which we will discuss in more depth in Chapter 3.
- You feel very uncomfortable being evaluated or watched when attempting to do something challenging and may mess it up because of your discomfort.
- You are easily distracted and affected by loud noises, other people, or stimuli like loud music and bright lights, thus finding it difficult to work in an office space with other people.
- You avoid situations that leave you feeling overwhelmed and are more affected by violence, conflict, and tension.
- You are prone to the stress of social comparison, feeling like you're behind everyone else. You feel like you hit your milestones later in life or undergo several career changes.

- You feel the negative or painful emotions of others as your own and may experience these emotions more deeply.
- Distractions and disruptions to your day are frustrating and unpleasant, and you may find it hard to bounce back or get back into your routine.
- You are prone to self-doubt and may remember an embarrassing mistake for a while, feeling even more ashamed for it than the average person would.
- You may be inclined to higher levels of depression and anxiety and feel socially awkward or anxious in large crowds or around people you don't know.

A HIGHLY SENSITIVE PERSON VS. AN EMPATH (ORLOFF, 2019)

The word empath has taken on a new meaning recently. At one point, it was mainly used in science fiction to describe someone with paranormal abilities who could understand the emotional and mental states of others. Nowadays, the word empath is a lot more mainstream and is used to describe someone who is extremely aware of the emotions of those around them.

An empath shares most of the traits of an HSP, like the need for more alone time, a low threshold to stimulation, aversion to large groups, and sensitivity to light, sound, and smell. It is likely that empaths will be highly sensitive and have gifts when it comes to processing life deeply. Empaths are attuned to other people's emotions and often have a "gut feeling or sixth sense" for subtleties in a group or between people. Empaths have great insight into themselves and others; however, they often feel and bear the burden of people's emotions more easily if they're not actively protecting themselves.

Empaths share the same rich inner life, love of nature and quiet environments that HSPs do. Empaths also have a desire to help others. However, empaths experience high sensitivity a lot more than HSPs. They absorb the energy from different environments and other people, whether positive or negative, whereas HSPs don't typically absorb another person's energy. If empaths aren't protecting themselves, when they absorb the energy, they energetically internalize the pain and emotions of others. For empaths, this ability is both a gift and a curse, and they often have difficulty distinguishing their own discomfort from someone else's. Many empaths also have a profound intuitive and spiritual experience with nature, animals, or their inner guides, which isn't usually associated with an HSP.

Empaths may not always have an explanation for how they're feeling. They may feel deep sadness or heaviness, only to find out later that one of their co-workers experienced a loss, and the empath is absorbing that person's emotions.

Being an empath and an HSP are not mutually exclusive. It is possible to be both, and many HSPs are also empaths. Suppose you think about the distinction in terms of the empathic spectrum. Empaths are on the far end of the scale. HSPs are a little further in. People who have empathy but are not HSPs or empaths are in the middle. And sociopaths, narcissists, and psychopaths with 'empath-deficient disorders' are on the opposite end of the scale.

How do introverts differ? (Wright, 2020)

Being an introverted person is genetic and involves differences in how the brain processes dopamine, the reward chemical. Introverts don't feel rewarded by external stimuli like crowds, small talk, or parties. As a result, their energy is depleted by these situations relatively quickly. Instead, introverted people find deep satisfaction from meaningful activities like reading, nature, creative hobbies, and quiet contemplation.

Lately, a lot of awareness has been raised around how introverts function. And most people now understand that being an introvert doesn't necessarily make you withdrawn or shy. Many introverts are social people and love spending time with a few close friends. However, social situations drain introverts quickly, so they need plenty of time alone to recharge their energy. For this reason, introverts may prefer to stay in or spend time with one or two close friends.

About 70% of highly sensitive people are introverts, so, understandably, these two traits are often confused. A highly sensitive introvert can be very caring, emotional, observant, and able to read others well, even though people exhaust them.

It is also possible to be an introvert and not be an HSP. This type of person would be less in tune with other people and less stressed by other stimuli like violent movies, time pressure, repetitive noises, or bright lights.

INTROVERT, HSP, OR EMPATH? (CROSTHWAITE, 2020)

Have a look at the following groups of questions:

Group One

1. You prefer small intimate groups or to be alone rather than in larger groups.
2. You have a few very good friends; you prefer quality over quantity.
3. You are perceived as being quiet and shy, even if that is not true.
4. Social situations can be very draining, and you often feel the need to retreat to recover.

Group Two

1. You find it difficult to make decisions, even small ones that may take very little effort.
2. You find it overwhelming to hear two sounds at once, like two people talking simultaneously or music playing while the television is on.
3. You find yourself becoming emotional very quickly, even about something as meaningless as a TV commercial.

4. You find it difficult to say no to people and overextend yourself to accommodate others, even to your own detriment.

Group Three

1. You find it easy to read people and know when they are holding back or lying to you.
2. After spending small amounts of time with people, you take on their personality traits, begin to speak like them or feel emotions they may be experiencing.
3. You feel physically ill or attacked during conflict.
4. After spending time with someone, you have to disconnect from them to get back to yourself and your own thoughts and feelings.

Do you find you resonate more with one specific group?

If you said a resounding YES to all of the questions in Group One, you show signs of being an introvert. In Group Two, you have traits of an HSP, and in Group Three, you have empathic tendencies. If you said yes to everything, you are probably a very sensitive person, and you will find a lot of help and understanding in the following chapters. If you didn't answer with many yesses, it doesn't mean you are not a highly sensitive person. You will learn so much more about yourself as we make our way through the pages of this book.

Being an HSP does not mean there's something wrong —it simply means that we process sensory data more deeply than others. While being an HSP has its drawbacks, it also has some wonderful and unique advantages. Recognizing that you're a highly sensitive person is the first step to embracing who you are and learning to better care for yourself.

In the next chapter, we will dive into why you are the way you are as an HSP. We will discuss why HSPs feel everything so strongly and why certain tasks are more challenging for you.

CHAPTER TWO

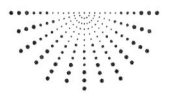

WHY YOU ARE THE WAY YOU ARE

There may have been a time in your life, or it may be an ever-present feeling, where you begrudge this innate trait of yours. There is absolutely nothing wrong with questioning being an HSP. On the contrary, it is a part of the journey toward self-acceptance. As a fellow HSP, I am often plagued by questions of how to exist, never mind thrive, in such a loud and clamorous world. I have often felt myself wishing there was an off switch. As the late Waylon Jennings sang, "Stop the world and let me off." Truthfully, it can be very overwhelming to feel everything so intensely. It can get lonely living in a world that neither understands nor speaks your language.

Over the years, I have come to realize what a powerful advantage high sensitivity can be. Today, as someone trained in spiritual therapies and trauma-informed care, empathy is a huge part of my job description, and I view my sensitivity as a gift. Although I have seen the upside, there are still some days when it's a struggle. I used to beat myself up about my sensitivity and always felt like I was operating by a different set of rules. I have come to realize that is a common experience for highly sensitive people; internally struggling with low self-esteem and self-doubt because we feel broken.

We are all currently living through cruel and unprecedented times. For an HSP, the news hits us harder than most, like a baseball bat to the back. But we are not broken or flawed. Our high sensory processing is an innate attribute, a gift to be treasured, no matter what society tells us. We possess the capacity to tune in and perceive what other people often miss.

Sensitive people attempt to fill the world with compassion for the good of others and, ultimately ourselves. This is a huge benefit in a world that believes dominance is somehow better than sensitivity. Good people gravitate toward us. Troubled people also gravitate toward us, often subconsciously seeking healing. One of the greatest benefits of being an HSP is that we can become a hub for amazing things. We make good leaders, and people may feel more creative under our influence, freer, and more comfortable with expressing their true selves. We need to use our gift of sensitivity to illuminate the dark corners of a world that needs healing.

We need to embrace the loneliness and honor the feeling. It is in the depths of solitude that we find the hidden treasures within us; however, remember that you are not alone. Reach out and connect. We need to find our soul family, iridescent people who feel like home. It is not easy, but we need to accept ourselves as we are. Being an HSP is a fantastic gift. Our high sensitivity means we have the potential to live an extraordinarily rich and meaningful life. We should not spend our days apologizing for who we are. You are a lighthouse, so let your light pierce through the darkness and stop saying sorry for shining so brightly!

WHY DO HIGHLY SENSITIVE PEOPLE FEEL EVERYTHING SO STRONGLY? (DANIELS, 2021)

The brain of an HSP may be one of the most powerful social machines in the known universe. Our brains notice little details about our surroundings that others miss, especially details about other people around us. We can process and feel everything a lot more strongly and deeply than others.

There are some key differences between a typical brain and the brain of an HSP.

1. Our brain responds differently to dopamine.

Dopamine, the reward chemical in the brain, drives us to want to do certain things, controls the pleasure we feel when we do them, and gives us a sense of victory. The genes involved with high sensitivity affect how our bodies use dopamine—in ways we don't completely understand yet. As highly sensitive people, we are less likely to be driven by external rewards than non-HSPs. These rewards are the "golden star stickers" of life, like a promotion, a new job, a monthly paycheck, or inclusion into a social group. HSPs are not as excited by the *things* many other people chase. The different use of dopamine in our bodies allows us to simply observe and be thoughtful while processing information. It also possibly is what prevents an HSP from being drawn into a highly stimulating environment that ends up overwhelming us. As an HSP, if you don't find yourself extremely drawn to a loud party or taking risks, you can thank your dopamine system for that.

2. We have more active mirror neurons.

Mirror neurons play a significant role in the brain of an HSP. They aid us in understanding what a person is experiencing or doing based on their actions. The mirror neurons are the brain cells that compare a person's behavior with previous situations where we behaved in that manner. The function of these neurons is to effectively mirror the person to figure out what is going on for them. This is an essential job for many reasons, but one of the main reasons is that it allows us to feel compassion and empathy for others. When we recognize the emotion someone is feeling, whether happiness or pain, we can relate to them thanks to these mirror neurons. The higher the mirror neuron activity, the more empathetic a person is—like an HSP. We don't necessarily have more mirror neurons than the typical brain; rather, our mirror neuron system is more active. As an HSP, these neurons are our super-power and sometimes our nemesis (like not being able to watch the same TV series as the rest of the family because it's too violent). However, the higher activity in our mirror neurons makes us caring, warm, and insightful about the needs of others.

3. We really do experience more vivid emotions.

There is an area in the front of the brain called the ventromedial prefrontal cortex (vmPFC). This area is associated with several systems in the body involving our values and emotions and processing sensory data. When we say an HSP feels everything more strongly than others, it's highly likely to happen here in the vmPFC. While the role of this area of the brain is not completely understood yet, it is definitely connected to our emotional regulation. It enhances the aspects we experience with *emotional vividness*. Life is generally experienced more vividly during emotional moments, not only by HSPs but by everyone. However, high sensitivity is linked to a gene that turns up this dial and increases this vividness. The highly sensitive gene allows emotional enhancement to have a much larger effect on the vmPFC as it processes our experiences. What does that mean for us highly sensitive people? This emotional vividness isn't social like the mirror neuron system. It's about how vividly we feel the emotions inside us in response to the environment around us. So, if you feel emotions more strongly than other people do, it's not just in your head (although it is, but you know what I mean). The HSP brain is finely tuned to pick up subtle emotional cues and react to them.

4. Other people are the brightest things on our radars.

For those who are less sensitive, it's easier to tune other people out. However, for HSPs, almost every part of our brain is wired to notice and interpret other people. This tendency is clear from the many imaging studies (Acevedo et al., 2014) done on the HSP brain. Certain studies (Acevedo et al., 2014) have also shown an increase in activity in the insula and the cingulate area. These two areas form our base for consciousness and awareness. In HSPs, these areas are a lot more active when responding to images of other people, especially when they're showing an emotion. In other words, HSPs are more conscious and alert in a social context.

These differences in the HSP brain are why we feel emotions a lot more strongly than the typical person. Although this part of the chapter is quite scientific, isn't it a relief to know that your emotions and feelings are completely valid?

WHY DO HSPS SEEM INTROVERTED, EVEN IF THEY'RE NOT?

Introverts and HSPs have many traits in common. About 70% of highly sensitive people are introverts, meaning a good number *are* actually extroverts. However, an introvert is not necessarily always an HSP (Sólo, 2020).

Let's have a look at what it means to be an introvert. Being introverted is often misunderstood and doesn't mean what people assume it does; it is an inherent biological variance that determines how people react to certain scenarios and how they unwind afterward. Many introverts enjoy social events just as much as extroverts do; they just approach them differently. An introvert gains enough stimulation from talking to a few people, while an extrovert is stimulated by moving around the party and meeting as many people as possible. The introvert becomes exhausted and overstimulated a lot faster than an extrovert, which is why they need to retreat and recharge with some alone time. This necessity is referred to as the *introvert hangover*. Introverts are not necessarily super sensitive to other people's emotions and the subtle cues around them. They are just quickly exhausted by large volumes of interaction with other people and need to recharge alone.

A few traits overlap between introverts and HSPs, which is why the two are often assumed to be the same. And this is why you seem introverted, even if you're not (Fraga, 2019).

1. You begin to feel unresponsive, overwhelmed, and tired after you've been out and about for too long. You withdraw a lot and need plenty of downtime, which often requires solitude. You find yourself retreating to a quiet room at the end of a long day—to soothe your senses, recharge, and lower your stimulation level.
2. You think deeply and may have been called an *old soul.* You process the information around you intensely and do a lot of reflecting on your experiences. This also means you're more prone to negative overthinking and spiral into anxious thoughts or obsessively play events over and over in your head. You have a constant internal monologue.
3. You notice the details that other people don't. Constantly being stimulated by your surroundings means that you have a keen eye for detail. You're seen as insightful and perceptive, and as a child, you may have been wise beyond your years.

4. You observe every situation and watch from the sidelines, making mental notes before speaking or involving yourself in a social situation. This observation allows you to prepare yourself to enter a conversation confidently, without stumbling over your words or doubting what you say. People are often drawn to you and tell you you're a good listener.
5. Loud noises and crowded environments can often feel overwhelming, and you've been told you look uncomfortable. Open office environments also drive you crazy, and you would much rather work from home.

WHY DO HSPS FEEL DIFFERENT OR ODD?

Before discovering that an HSP is a coined term and that my brain functions differently, I always felt like something was wrong with me. Sadly, this feeling was enforced by some of the people around me. Perhaps while growing up, you were asked, "Why are you so sensitive? Lighten up!" Or maybe you were told, "Don't be so sensitive; you're being silly!" Telling an HSP not to be sensitive is like saying, "Don't have such blue eyes."

In reality, we don't choose to have a highly sensitive temperament any more than we choose the color of our eyes, our height, or our predisposition to an illness. What makes matters worse is that most of the world is socialized to see sensitivity as a weakness, to the extent that we HSPs begin to believe that it's a weakness and, therefore, struggle with self-esteem. Highly sensitive children are often subject to hearing: "Toughen up," "Get over it," or "Shake it off!"

Of course, all HSPs differ slightly, and not all of us have the same characteristics. Some HSPs are brought to tears by a beautiful song or the innocence of a newborn baby. Others, myself included, cringe and feel physical pain when faced with the sight of abuse. Torture scenes in movies are unbearable for most of us, even though we are fully aware that the events are not real. This unexplainable and strong reaction to both violence and beauty is one of the challenges that only HSPs truly understand.

One out of five people is highly sensitive (Aron), leaving four out of five unaware of hypersensitivity. Many people don't mean to be insensitive; they just haven't been educated and don't fully understand what it's like to be an HSP. Many people are under the impression that sensitivity is "learned or taught" and that it's not an innate trait like having blonde hair.

WHY DO HSPS STRUGGLE TO SAY NO? (TRITTIN, 2018)

As an HSP, saying no is one of the biggest struggles I'm faced with. Even when I want to say no, I find myself saying yes to a friend who wants to hang out. I can't help but answer my work emails during odd hours if someone says it's urgent. I can't restrain myself from shuffling my schedule around to accommodate one more person. The only problem is, by saying yes to everyone else, I'm saying no to myself.

This is a common HSP problem. In general, HSPs struggle with saying no. Saying yes to people and putting them first makes us feel like good partners or friends. Not only does saying yes to everything make us feel good about ourselves, but the other people in our lives love it and may begin to encourage it. Whether it be conscious or unconscious, they may start taking advantage of us. This behavior results in HSPs being walked over and ending up emotionally and physically exhausted. I often find myself wishing that others could pick up on my cues of wanting to say no and let me off the hook easily. I can promise you this is not an effective strategy!

There are various reasons we as HSPs struggle to say no, especially to our loved ones. The overarching reason is empathy. Not only do we have the capacity to put ourselves in someone's shoes and imagine what they're feeling, but we actually absorb the emotions other people are emitting and feel them as if they were our own. Empathy is a gift, but it can lead to our downfall. We need to be able to turn it off if necessary. Empathy directly results in us being unable to say no because we see and feel that the other person wants us to say yes. This makes us desperately want to say yes as well. The other person's desire becomes our own feeling. To say no, we need to set our minds to ignore that absorbed emotion, which is not an easy task.

Although many other people experience the fear of rejection, HSPs are terrified of it. The fear of abandonment is one of the most common fears amongst humans. If we consider our survival instincts, this fear makes sense because isolation kills. HSPs often crave a deep connection with other people, so the absence of that connection has a more significant effect on us. By always saying yes, we leave less room for abandonment than if we say no. Saying yes is a way to feel safer in our relationships with others. We also tend to feel hurt or offended more easily and have a habit of taking things personally. If someone told us no, we might take that as a personal slam, so we avoid doing the same to other people. HSPs can't stand making other people upset or hurting their feelings. Because of our fear of abandonment and empathy, we never want to be on the receiving end of anyone's negative emotions.

WHY IS IT HARD FOR AN HSP TO SPEAK UP AND ASK FOR OUR NEEDS TO BE MET? (SAPALA, 2018)

I am 100% sure that I'm not the first HSP to struggle with speaking up, and I definitely won't be the last. The issue of speaking up for ourselves is not only difficult to do but often brings up emotional baggage from our past. For most HSPs, we feel that our personal needs are strange and inconvenient to other people. We need more time to process. We need more space than others. We need more depth and complexity. Other people often don't understand these needs and may feel rejected in some way. This leads to us learning that we should constantly compromise our needs.

As a result, instead of working on a way to negotiate our needs with others, we withdraw further into our own world. We attempt to meet our needs in our own space, completely by ourselves. This works half of the time, and the other half causes us to feel unheard, resentful, powerless, and isolated.

As an HSP, we have two choices. We can choose to acknowledge our needs and step into our personal power; this may mean being uncomfortable while speaking up for what we need. Or we can choose to be powerless, suppressing our needs and keeping quiet, which still guarantees that we will feel uncomfortable—and probably bitter, angry and exhausted, which commonly leads to burnout.

Most HSPs struggle with people-pleasing tendencies, which we will discuss more in Chapter 3. We always want to make sure that everyone in our surrounding environment is happy—especially with us. However, this is, unfortunately, a battle we will never win. It is impossible to be in charge of other people's emotions, nor should we be. We need to learn to step back and let people have their own reactions, even if that means they don't always feel positive toward us.

How to stop feeling responsible for the emotions of others

If you have people-pleasing tendencies and feel personally responsible for other people's emotions, especially when speaking up about your needs, this four-step process may offer some guidance (Sapala, 2018).

1. Evaluate your needs.

Does your need encroach on the rights of anyone else, or is it harmful to others? If you're not invading another person's space or being disrespectful of boundaries, it is safe to say you are justified in asking that your needs be met and respected. Of course, common sense should be used as well. If you can speak up for what you need and still be respectful of others, I encourage you to do it. It is definitely not your responsibility to set boundaries for others—only yourself.

2. Use your preferred method of communication.

Many HSPs have a misguided notion that we need to have face-to-face confrontations with people. I don't know about you, but nothing makes me feel like I want to crawl under a rock more than that thought. There is a solution, however. From this day forward, you have permission and should communicate your needs using your preferred method of communication whenever and to whomever you want without feeling guilty. If you feel you communicate more effectively in writing, then do so. Send that email to your co-worker or write that letter to your neighbor's mailbox.

3. Maintain your boundaries over time.

Even after you've identified your needs and have spoken up about them, other parties may still try and push your buttons. This behavior might be consciously manipulative or unconsciously oblivious. Asking once may not be enough. Sometimes, you need to reinforce your boundaries and go through the process again. The upside to this is that the more you have to do it, the more practice you gain in taking back your power.

4. Only hold responsibility for yourself.

There will be countless times when it feels easier to put another person's comfort before yours. When you're busy evaluating your needs, you may be tempted to push them aside so someone else can do what they want, and you can avoid any negative reaction from them. However, the reactions of others are not your responsibility. They have never been, and they never will be. You are only responsible for yourself, and you're not helping anyone by trying to manage other people's emotions.

Speaking up for ourselves and stating our needs is not easy, but it must be done if we are truly committed to thriving as HSPs. The more we practice doing it, the more we'll be able to readily identify our responsibility, what belongs to others, and how to draw the line between them. We will get to a place where we consistently step into our own power with purpose and passion.

HOW THE SUBCONSCIOUS BELIEFS OF AN HSP AFFECT OUR PERCEPTION AND INTERACTION WITH OTHERS

The concept of "nature versus nurture" is a long-standing debate amongst psychologists. What creates our behaviors? Is behavior biological, or is it based on what we learn from our environment? What causes a belief to continue, and what causes a generational pattern to cease?

Many HSPs feel like something is wrong with them and that they don't function normally. Often, their behavior not only results from the innate gene of high sensitivity but also the subconscious beliefs and patterns that have been ingrained in their minds.

HSPs are known to be observers and extremely sensitive to external stimuli, which means they are more affected by their surrounding environment than others. Regarding the *nature versus nurture* debate, HSPs are more deeply affected by the "nurture" aspect through what they witness and absorb around them. HSPs soak up any generational beliefs or patterns very quickly and easily. These beliefs or patterns are often accompanied by worry, fear, the need to please, take responsibility, or fix everyone.

The Subconscious Mind's Role in Unhealthy Patterns (Cole, 2021)

The subconscious mind is the part of us responsible for storing emotions and patterns. This subconscious mind is also the home to our core beliefs. If a parent or guardian held on to any of the following beliefs, it could be the reason why the patterns in your life reoccur from generation to generation:

- I am not worthy.
- People will abandon me if I can't make them happy.
- Life is always going to be a struggle.
- It's my responsibility to make others happy.
- I need to be perfect and have no flaws to be good enough for others.
- I can't have a healthy relationship.
- There is something wrong with me.

Some of these patterns may feel rather familiar to HSPs because of our extra sensitive souls. Unfortunately, our subconscious mind finds these beliefs familiar, even though they are unwanted and unhealthy.

Suppose you grew up in a dysfunctional family where you were the primary caretaker, or there was abuse. In that case, you may have adopted the subconscious belief that denying your own needs was the safest choice because it may have been dangerous to ask for what you needed. In my sessions where there is regression back to childhood, it is incredibly common for the client to go back to a trauma that led them to believe they were not important, not visible, or they are somehow different than others. These moments create a belief that they are simply not good enough and that their needs do not matter. These persistent beliefs ingrained from your childhood may be why you have toxic patterns in your life now, like constantly feeling the need to please others.

It is important not to blame yourself for these patterns and beliefs and to know that you have the power to break them. The first step is becoming aware of them and becoming self-disciplined about the new, healthier choices you're making.

If you notice unhealthy patterns in yourself, here are some things you can do:

1. Do not blame yourself.

It is essential to take a step back and acknowledge the pattern or belief in a nonjudgmental way. Don't allow yourself to be caught up in the pattern. This can be hard for highly sensitive people because they often feel the need to take ownership and responsibility for themselves. However, noticing and even naming the belief or pattern is the first step to breaking it. You may say, "I have noticed this pattern of having an awful relationship with my money. I noticed it with the way my parents dealt with money, and now I notice it in myself. It is time for me to change this pattern. I choose to change now."

2. Get clear on how to break the pattern and focus on how to be self-disciplined about your new choices.

Get clear on the new pattern you want to create. What are the tell-tale signs of the old pattern reemerging? This often involves the things or people you need to say no to. Saying no can be difficult for an HSP, but breaking the unhealthy belief or pattern is essential. For example, if you're looking to find a healthy relationship with a new partner, get clear on your definition of a healthy relationship. What are the common themes with your previous relationships that you refuse to accept now? Practice saying no and setting boundaries for yourself. The more consistent you are with your new choices, the easier it will become. The meditation included at the beginning of this book will assist you in this process.

3. Work on forgiveness.

Forgiving doesn't mean excusing the behavior of those who continued the unhealthy belief or pattern but rather allows you to let go of any negative feelings you are still holding on to. When doing forgiveness work, imagine that the anger you're holding on to is a piece of hot coal; it is only hurting you. By letting go of any resentful feelings, you are choosing to create a new and healthier belief.

4. Work with a therapist.

Seeking professional help will allow you to work deeply around your core beliefs and focus on self-love. Working with a therapist will help you change your unconscious beliefs and current mindset. This journey is about feeling empowered and worthy. It is about having support as you choose to change your life, as well as future generations to come.

MISCONCEPTIONS ABOUT HSPS

Being highly sensitive comes with its perks and drawbacks. You will understand what I'm talking about if you're an HSP. HSPs are a misunderstood group. We're often treated as though we're weak when we are really strong for holding so many feelings. These myths about HSPs can damage other people's perceptions of us and get in the way of us exploring our authentic selves.

As a highly sensitive soul, I would like to clear up some misconceptions about HSPs. Here are a few of them:

1. **Being an HSP is not a medical condition or disorder that needs to be "fixed." (Sólo, 2018)** Being highly sensitive is an innate trait in a fifth of the population and many other nonhuman species. Being sensitive is desperately needed in our society, and the world might be a better place if there were more HSPs in it.
2. **Being an HSP is not the same as being introverted (Mueller, 2017).** Many HSPs keep to themselves because settings with large crowds overwhelm them. However, that does not mean they don't enjoy the company of others or aren't extroverted by nature. You can be an HSP and an extrovert; about a third of HSPs are actually extroverts.
3. **Sensitivity is not the same thing as weakness (Mueller, 2017).** Being highly sensitive does not mean being unable to handle what life throws at you. It does mean that you're absorbing more than others—if you can handle that, you're truly very strong. An HSP needs harmony in their

life, which often means avoiding conflict or highly competitive situations. Competitive people may see this as weak, but it's actually a more thoughtful approach that creates a solution that works for everybody.

4. **Being highly sensitive does not mean being full of drama (Sólo, 2018).** People who get offended easily are always told not to be *so sensitive*. However, high sensitivity has nothing to do with getting offended, overreacting, or creating drama. It simply means that you process everything deeply.

5. **HSPs are not on the autism spectrum (Weiss, 2018).** High sensitivity and autism can be merged, but they are also two very different things. Many HSPs do not have autism, and although autistic people can be sensitive, so can anyone else.

6. **HSPs are not outwardly emotional (Weiss, 2018).** An HSP may feel a lot of emotion inside, but they will often suppress it. You cannot necessarily tell an HSP from a non-HSP just by observing them. Highly sensitive people do not cry at everything. Yes, they feel emotions more strongly, but they have also learned how to handle their tears and control their emotions to avoid disrupting others.

7. **HSPs automatically have low self-esteem (Mueller, 2017).** This misconception comes from the fact that HSPs tend to apologize a lot; this is not because of low self-esteem but rather because they sense everything, even the smallest negative emotion. Their natural response is to say, "I'm sorry."
8. **HSPs are not only women (Weiss, 2018).** Women are always stereotyped as more sensitive than men, but men are equally sensitive—they just tend to hold their emotions in. Our culture has taught men to express sensitivity differently.
9. **Being an HSP does not mean being uptight (Mueller, 2017).** As a kid in school, sitting next to another child that loved clicking their pen or knocking on the desk all day could cause a sudden urge to scream, "Stop it!" Despite what this looks like, it's not uptight. Every sense is magnified for an HSP, so it's very easy to get overstimulated by a repetitive noise.
10. **Being an HSP does not mean being a baby about pain (Mueller, 2017).** Heightened pain means physical pain too. HSPs aren't just crying for attention; it really does hurt.

Being a highly sensitive person is a unique trait to live with, and although it has its ups and downs, I bet most HSPs would not trade their higher sensitivity if they had the chance. Personally, I believe I would be a completely different person if I weren't an HSP—and I definitely wouldn't want that! Many challenges come with being an HSP, but the upsides make it worthwhile. We can learn to thrive.

In Chapter 3, we will discuss why HSPs are prone to people-pleasing and how to break that cycle.

CHAPTER THREE

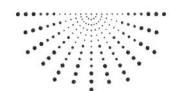

PLEASE STOP PLEASING

There is a difference between a peacemaker and a people-pleaser. A peacemaker wants to reach a resolution and restore balance. They try to see the issue from all sides objectively and rationally. A peacemaker wants to help others, even if it means telling the truth, which may hurt. They tell it like it is, even if the people involved don't want to face reality.

On the other hand, a people-pleaser wants everyone around them to be happy, so they will basically do whatever anyone asks of them. Saying yes to people may be a habit for some people-pleasers, while for others, it has become an addiction that makes them feel as though they are needed. Constantly saying yes to others makes the people-pleaser feel useful and important—like they're adding value to someone else's life.

Being a people-pleaser also comes from the need to create an interpersonal bridge to others. This bridge is our connection with other people through various types of bonds or shared experiences. Typically, this bridge is created through family relationships, school, work activities, being neighborly, common interests, sharing similar values, or having relatable life experiences.

HIGHLY SENSITIVE PEOPLE AND PEOPLE-PLEASING (GRANNEMAN, 2014)

Being a highly sensitive person makes being a people-pleaser even more complicated. In general, our relationships are more challenging because our values differ greatly from those around us. When it comes to relationships, we may even feel disadvantaged because we are not competitive and seek mutuality, not a contest. As HSPs, we often fail to get the respect we deserve because our empathy and kindness are not valued. HSPs feel like they don't belong with other people. We experience the world so differently and may fail to develop interpersonal bridges. This leaves us feeling lonely and misunderstood, which results in us turning to people-pleasing to get the social acceptance we are craving.

Our need to people-please surfaces when trying to fit in with a group, like a work environment or family. We want to gain some social standing, but they are different from us. In any scenario, people-pleasing comes from thinking that the responsibility to build the interpersonal bridge is ours. Unless we put in a lot more effort, a connection may not form.

HSPs are also likely to be people-pleasers because we dislike conflict. We are worried that if we say no to someone or speak our mind, we'll cause the other person to feel disappointed or hurt. Before we even get a chance to say no, our minds run away with us, creating scenarios of the uncomfortable situations that could occur. HSPs read other people easily, so we pick up on subtle displeasure or anger (or perhaps we imagine the other person is unhappy). This causes us to feel guilty or ashamed, and we end up saying yes. We also find it difficult to accept criticism, and people-pleasing is a way to avoid being criticized.

When we feel the need to people-please, we are doing more than necessary in our relationships. People-pleasing puts us in a position where we feel inferior to the other person in some way. It is how we hide our "different-ness" and a way for us to survive in a social environment where we feel disadvantaged.

Causes of people-pleasing (Cherry)

Various factors may play a role in people-pleasing:

1. **Poor self-esteem.** People are often people-pleasers because they don't value their own needs and desires. A lack of self-confidence causes a need for external validation, and people-pleasers feel that saying yes to others and doing favors will lead to acceptance and approval.
2. **Insecurity.** In other cases, people might turn into people-pleasers because they are worried that people won't like or accept them if they don't go above and beyond to make others happy.
3. **Perfectionism.** Some people want everything to be "just right' which includes how other people think and feel.
4. **Past experiences.** Traumatic, difficult, or painful experiences may also play a part in people-pleasing. People who have suffered through abuse or rejection may try to please others to avoid conflict or feel abandoned. They

will try everything possible to make other people happy to avoid triggering abusive behavior.

Effects of being a people-pleaser (Cerbo, 2016)

Being a people-pleaser isn't always a bad thing. Being a caring and concerned person is an important part of maintaining a healthy relationship. However, it becomes a problem when you're trying to win approval or are pursuing happiness at the expense of your own emotional and mental well-being.

The following are some of the effects of being a people-pleaser:

1. **Anger and Frustration.** While you may enjoy helping others, you are also bound to experience some anger or frustration when you're doing things out of obligation or reluctance. These negative feelings can lead to a cycle of helping a person, feeling anger or frustration toward them for taking advantage, and then feeling regretful or sorry for yourself.
2. **Anxiety and Stress.** Constantly keeping others happy can stretch your own mental, emotional, and physical resources too thin. Trying to manage how people feel can leave you with

nothing but stress and anxiety, which can detrimentally affect your health.

3. **Depleted Willpower.** With all your energy and mental resources spent on making sure other people are happy, you have less willpower to tackle your own goals and care for your own needs. Willpower and self-control may be limited resources, according to recent studies (Cherry, 2021). Spending all your willpower on others leaves you with little left to devote to yourself.
4. **Lack of Authenticity.** People-pleasers often hide their own needs, opinions, or preferences to accommodate others. This will make you feel like you're not living an authentic life, almost like you don't really know who you are.
5. **Weaker Relationships.** The people in your life may appreciate your giving nature, but at some point, they may also begin to take your kindness and willingness to help for granted. People may not even realize they're taking advantage of you. They just know you're always willing to help, so they do not doubt that you'll be there whenever help is needed. What they might not see is how overcommitted and thinly stretched you may be. Putting in all of your efforts to meet other

people's expectations may leave you feeling resentful.

HOW PEOPLE-PLEASING AFFECTS YOUR RELATIONSHIPS

Throughout my early life, most of my relationships have been one-sided; I, the giver of my time, and others happy to receive my generosity. I never questioned this imbalance because, in my mind, it was simply the way the world worked. I always said yes and was continually exhausted, overwhelmed, overcommitted, and miserable.

One day I noticed a recurring theme in my life–resentment. In general, the feeling that followed my inability to say no was resentment. My overgiving led to me feeling resentful toward the people in my life.

People-pleasing in relationships might seem like a good thing. After all, when you're with someone, supporting them and making them happy is important. As a people-pleaser, you're doing both, right? Maybe. However, you are probably often doing it at your own expense. By people-pleasing, you may not only lose touch with your own preferences and needs but also have a buildup of silent resentment. Instead of voicing your feelings, you end up holding on to anger that your partner isn't even aware of, all because you're trying to avoid conflict.

Over time, the resentment and unhappiness could lead to you seeking a connection elsewhere or abruptly leaving the relationship. All while your partner wasn't even aware there was a problem.

Here are some of the ways people-pleasing may be hurting your relationships:

1. If we are the ones doing everything for our family members, friends, and co-workers, they are not going to experience growth. By always being available to help, we limit their ability to take on new tasks. When we're not around, they might not complete the tasks successfully because they may not know what to do on their own.
2. Our people-pleasing habits deny other people the opportunity to help us and love us equitably. If the people in your life don't know your needs, they can't fulfill them.
3. By constantly people-pleasing, our actions create indebtedness. This is not something that is verbally agreed upon but makes others feel like they're held hostage and need to repay us for our sacrifice.

4. People-pleasing relationships are often based on dishonesty (or, at the very least, not full disclosure). This means the connection we have with others isn't always real. If we cannot be honest about what we want in a relationship, give our opinion during a conversation, or discuss what truly brings us joy, our partner won't know who we truly are. It also makes it difficult for anyone to know how to love us. When our communications are only partial truths or our interactions are dishonest or incomplete, it degrades the trust and connection between the other person and us. Our relationships may lack authenticity.

WHY PEOPLE-PLEASING IS SO DANGEROUS FOR HSPS (CERBO, 2016)

People-pleasing often has the opposite effect than what is intended. We, as people-pleasers, may strive to get a positive reaction from others, but instead, we make people feel subtly uneasy. So why is being super attentive and self-sacrificing met with awkwardness and avoidance? Why does this result in people feeling uneasy instead of grateful? Well, it activates a "spider-sense" in most people and leaves others subconsciously wondering, "Why is this person so concerned with how

I feel? Why are they so eager to please? Are they hiding something?"

Someone without any visible wants or needs doesn't seem right. It is also impossible not to have wants and needs. This is why people may feel uneasy around us. When we go into a people-pleasing mode, which is essentially to hide our true selves, other people may feel wary around us. Often, they don't even understand why. This results in them subtly withdrawing from us, and because of our heightened perception, this rejection can be painful.

Unfortunately, most highly sensitive people respond to rejection and social awkwardness by people-pleasing even more. This results in a vicious cycle of people-pleasing followed by exhaustion, defeat, and intense feelings of rejection. It becomes completely overwhelming—yet it is so hard to stop pleasing everyone.

WHY IS IT DIFFICULT TO STOP PEOPLE-PLEASING? (MATHEWS, 2015)

The short answer is that people-pleasing is a defense mechanism. It is a strategy for protection. It is a way for people to adapt when faced with a difficult or uncomfortable situation.

At the core, people-pleasers are afraid of rejection. Everyone fears rejection, but rejection is worse for HSPs. Often people-pleasing is connected to trauma. In some cases, a people-pleaser may have experienced rejection from their caregivers on enough occasions to doubt the constancy of other people's love. They feel like they need to perform or earn love by behaving in helpful or pleasing ways. In practice, this rejection could look like a breakup or a fallout between two close friends. It could be something more subtle, like getting the silent treatment from a family member for days or weeks at a time. People-pleasers often grow up in households where affection and love are based on performance. This isn't only academic or athletic performance; it can be performing by doing what they're told. For example, in one household, the unspoken rule might be to show very little emotion. This sort of "pull yourself together" mentality is a form of rejection. So the unspoken rule in this family would be something like: "Don't talk about what you're feeling, and we'll get along just fine." Anyone who breaks this rule gets branded as a drama queen, too emotional, too sensitive, or too much. All of these labels are a form of rejection and judgment.

Most people-pleasers I know have been labeled as *'too much.'* The sad paradox of this situation is that highly sensitive people's "undesired or unpleasant" feelings will be heightened in a family like the above example. This just brings about a cycle of rejection and conflict. The person's feelings will be soothed when they are compassionately acknowledged, and that generally comes from doing something that makes someone happy, aka people-pleasing.

In another family, the unspoken rule may have to do with achievement and excellence. If the child is at the top of their class or performs well, they receive love. A child in this family develops performance-based self-esteem. Essentially, all of their feelings of self-worth come from what they do rather than who they are. While this person may be a shining star, they don't have a sense of their own intrinsic self-worth. They learn that taking risks is a no-go, and their creativity and voice are often stifled by fear of failure and ultimately being rejected for failing.

A person from a family like this has never had the necessary safety to explore their own preferences or creativity. They were always too busy trying to *take the temperature of the room*. They always had to figure out what others were feeling and in need of to anticipate and take care of those needs. This is often referred to as parentification by therapists. This is when a child or teenager takes on the role of soothing, nurturing, or tending to their parents or other adults in hopes they will receive praise.

Children who grow up to be people-pleasers live with a threat hanging over them—the threat of rejection. The threat of "or else": *"Do this or else I won't love you anymore."* And if the child does the opposite of what is expected, they experience rejection.

Another reason people find it hard to break the people-pleasing cycle is because when they do something that makes others happy, they receive positive reinforcement. This does a great job of boosting their confidence and performance-based self-esteem (at least for a little while). Other people get to benefit from all their generosity, and they get a confidence boost. However, the admiration is short-lived, and once it wears off, they feel the need to people-please again.

Often, people find it hard to stop people-pleasing because there is no clear alternative. Even if a person is able to work through their fear of conflict and rejection, the crippling guilt that comes with setting boundaries and many other hallmark features of this behavior is challenging to overcome. People-pleasers often default to being caregivers and pleasing others because they haven't had the safety or space to figure out an alternative way of being in the world. Breaking free from being a people-pleaser takes effort and a multifaceted approach. Numerous aspects need to be addressed to truly take your power back. The good news is that it is all completely possible!

BREAKING FREE FROM PEOPLE-PLEASING (CHERRY)

People-pleasing is a behavior that can be challenging to overcome. Fortunately, there are some steps you can take to stop being a people-pleaser. You can learn how to balance your desire to make others happy without sacrificing your own needs.

1. Establish boundaries.

It is important to know your limits, establish clear boundaries, and then be willing to communicate those limits and boundaries. Be specific and clear about what you are willing to take on. If it feels like someone is asking for too much from you, let them know it is over the bounds of what you are willing to do, and you won't be able to help them. There are also some other ways to create boundaries in your life to help overcome your people-pleasing tendencies. For example, setting limitations on when you're able to talk and only answering your phone during certain times.

2. Start small.

Changing a behavioral pattern can be difficult. It can be challenging to make a sudden change to your people-pleasing habits, so it is often easier to start asserting yourself in small ways. In many scenarios, you have to learn to restrain yourself as well as work on teaching the people around you to respect your limits. This is a lot to do all in one go, so it can be helpful to start with some small steps that help you work toward being less of a people-pleaser. Begin by saying no to smaller requests, ask for something you need, or try expressing your opinion about something small. For example, start by saying no to a request via text. Then work your way up to saying *no* in person. Practice this in different scenarios or settings, like when ordering at a restaurant, talking to a salesperson, or dealing with a co-worker. It also helps to start setting boundaries with people who are more likely to respect them. Create positive experiences by starting with smaller, easier ones that will teach your nervous system and mind that this is a safe and healthy practice.

3. Set goals and priorities.

Think about where you want to spend your time and energy. What goals are you aiming to accomplish? Who do you want to help? When you know your priorities, you will be able to determine if you have the time and energy to devote to something. If you find that something or someone is draining your energy or using too much of your time, take the necessary steps to address the problem. When you begin putting your boundaries into practice and saying no to the things you don't want to do, you will find you have more time and energy to devote to the important things in your life.

4. Stall for time.

When someone asks you for a favor, tell them you need time to think about it. You can respond with, "Let me get back to you on that" or "I don't have my calendar on me; let me check when I get a minute." Saying yes straight away may leave you feeling obligated and overcommitted. However, taking the time to respond to someone's request will give you the time you need to think it through and decide if it's something you would like to take on. Before you make the decision, ask yourself:

- How stressed will I be if I say yes?
- How much time is this going to take?
- Do I have the time to do it?
- Is it something I really want to do?

- Will this be uplifting or draining?

Research has also shown that even a short pause (and a deep breath) before deciding increases decision-making accuracy. When you give yourself a moment, it will be easier for you to accurately decide if it's a task you have time for and wish to take on.

5. Assess the request.

Another step you can take toward overcoming your people-pleasing trait is to look for any sign that someone may be trying to take advantage of your generosity. Is the request coming from someone who always seems to want something from you but is suddenly unavailable when you need them to return the favor? Are some people aware of your generous nature and ask because they know you won't say no? If you feel like you are being manipulated into doing something, take the time to assess what you're being asked to do and decide how you want to handle the request. If someone keeps taking advantage of your kindness and insisting you should help, be firm and clear about your decision not to help.

6. Avoid making excuses.

It is vital to be direct when you say no and don't blame other obligations or make excuses for your inability to help or take on the task. When you start explaining why you can't do something, you give other people the chance to poke holes through your excuse. Explaining your reason behind saying no also gives them the chance to change their request to ensure you can still do what they're asking. Try and use a decisive tone when you say no to something and resist the urge to add unnecessary detail about your reasoning. Remember, *"No"* is a complete sentence.

7. Relationships require *give and take*.

A secure and healthy relationship involves a certain degree of mutuality. If one person is constantly giving and the other is always taking, it often means one of them is forgoing their needs to ensure the other person has what they want. Even if you enjoy making other people happy, it is important to remember that they should also be giving to you in return.

8. Create a mantra.

Create an empowering mantra and stick it somewhere you will see it often, like on your mirror, as a background on your phone, or next to your computer. This mantra will act as a mini pep talk throughout the day. Here are a few to try:

- I am allowed to say no
- A no to them is a yes to me
- "No" is a complete sentence
- Not my circus, not my monkeys (always makes me giggle)
- I don't owe anyone an explanation
- I am the guardian of my time and energy

9. Say no with conviction.

As a people-pleaser, you may be tempted to say "maybe" or "I don't know" to an invitation, even though you're not interested. Instead, use an effective and polite way to decline. If saying the word "no" outright seems a bit harsh, try one of these:

- Unfortunately, I'm at full capacity.
- I won't be able to make it.
- I'll have to pass on that project.

- I have plans that day but thank you for thinking of me.
- I am honored, but someone else will be more suited to dedicate the time that deserves.

10. Sit with the discomfort.

For most people, especially HSPs, people-pleasing is a way to alleviate the intense feelings of discomfort when it comes to rejection, feeling less-than-perfect, or abandonment. However, if you learn to sit with those uncomfortable feelings and breathe through them, they will have less power over your actions.

11. Help when you want to help.

Overcoming your people-pleasing tendencies doesn't mean you need to give up being thoughtful and kind. These are all desirable qualities that contribute to stronger, lasting relationships. However, you need to examine your motivations and intentions. Don't only do things because you fear rejection or seek the approval of others. Continue doing good things but do them on your own terms. Being a kind person doesn't demand attention or rewards. It simply requires the desire to make things better for someone else but not at the expense of your happiness.

12. Examine why you feel compelled to please by journaling on these prompts.

The following questions will help you understand the root cause of your people-pleasing: (this will be incredibly eye-opening, grab a pen and paper and free write for at least 3 minutes per question; it will be worth it!)

- Which relationships make me feel the need to please people?
- How do I depend on other people for resources of any kind that cause me to be in a people-pleasing relationship?
- What changes do I need to make to reduce my dependency on others to have fewer relationships where I need to please?
- If I can't reduce my needs, what are the alternative solutions that support my self-respect?
- Am I able to create what I need?
- Am I able to ask for more of what I need from my one-sided relationships to create more mutuality?

13. Understand you can't control everything.

Let other people make their own choices and have their own reactions. It helps to accept that you cannot control other people's emotions. No matter what you do, someone is going to disapprove. You cannot win everyone over. It is better to let other people be and accept how they feel, even if it's a negative emotion toward you. At the end of the day, the only opinion about yourself that matters is yours.

14. Celebrate your progress.

Overcoming people-pleasing is hard work, and many people aren't willing to put in the effort and get uncomfortable. Take the time to celebrate your achievements, no matter how small. Keep a confidence file, which could be a list on your phone, of all the ways you are learning to stop people-pleasing. Each time you need a confidence boost, refer to it.

15. Seek professional support.

There is no shame in seeking the help of a professional. Trauma therapies like Eye Movement Desensitization and Reprocessing (EMDR), hypnotherapy, psychotherapy and counseling can help you process any traumatic memories that have caused the need for people-pleasing. Therapy can help eliminate any fear, anxiety, and guilt that comes with asking for help, requesting your needs to be met, or saying no to someone.

WRAPPING UP CHAPTER 3

Being a people-pleaser, especially as an HSP, can make it difficult to pursue your own happiness. Finding ways to overcome this behavior and setting boundaries to take back your time is important. Often the work that comes with overcoming people-pleasing tendencies involves figuring out the root cause. If you have experienced trauma or rejection in your life, it helps to work through these past hurts to free yourself.

Remind yourself daily that you can't please everyone. Accept that not everyone will share the same values as you, and that's okay. When you choose to stop chasing people to make them happy, you will have a lot more free time and energy to invest in the people who understand, accept, and appreciate you. It will take time, effort, and baby steps from your side, but the results will be worth it (trust me, I know).

In the next chapter, we are going to discuss the word *no*. It is your biggest weapon. We will cover the importance of saying no and work through some helpful tips on how to get comfortable saying it!

CHAPTER FOUR

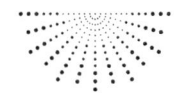

NO IS YOUR BIGGEST WEAPON

As we discussed in Chapter 3, HSPs feel the need to be of service. We are people-pleasers. We have a difficult time saying no to others. We find it tough to say no because we dislike confrontation. We find it easier to say yes to everyone and make them happy because that means there is a slim chance of any conflict breaking out. Always saying yes to people makes us feel like we're supportive and helpful. For a short period of time, their acknowledgment of our actions makes us feel happy and needed. The problem that comes with not being able to say no is that we end up wishing other people would reciprocate our actions, and we bottle up resentment toward them.

SAYING NO AS AN HSP (GRANNEMAN, 2014)

One of the hardest lessons I've had to learn in my life and career is the significance of saying no. The word *no* is not one that ever came naturally to me, as I suspect with many other HSPs. I was always eager to be a team player and lend a helping hand. It wasn't until I started to say no to projects, opportunities, and people that were not consistent with my core values and vision that I made significant strides in my life. Our ability to say no is a valuable skill. Without it, it's nearly impossible to achieve our visions and dreams.

So why is it so tough to say no as an HSP? There are various complicating factors. The biggest contributor to our struggle with saying no is because we feel everything very strongly. We also absorb the emotions of those around us and feel them as if they were our own. Our empathy and sensitivity pick up on the other person's emotions, and we can tell if they want us to say yes. The disappointment we imagine the other person will feel if we say no "guilts" us into saying yes because we don't want to upset other people. Because we're so sensitive when someone says no to us, it hurts more, and we take it personally. We also relate to people emotionally, so because we know how much being told no can hurt, we don't want to inflict that pain on others (even though a non-HSP probably wouldn't be too bothered).

We are terrified of rejection and conflict. If we say no to others, we risk upsetting them, which in our minds will lead to conflict. If we don't make them happy, we run the risk of them rejecting us. In the mind of an HSP, it is a catch-twenty-two situation. Saying yes to others instead of putting our needs first leaves less room for abandonment than saying no does.

HSPs are often told we are blessed because of our gifts and need to give back. We're made to feel like we owe the world because we were born with advantages thanks to our sensitivity. This feeling of owing everyone our time and skill doesn't help with saying no. We almost feel guilty because then we're denying people our service.

The people around us also consciously or unconsciously pick up on the fact that we're sensitive and willing to help. Often, they may take advantage, especially if you're in the wellness or hospitality industry. Family and friends may expect free treatments and assume you'll give it to them because of your generous nature. Clients may call out of office time in a crisis. Our inner need to selflessly help others means we are likely to give in to these people.

Not saying no may also be ingrained in some HSPs if they grew up in dysfunctional families. Saying no might have been dangerous in the case of an abusive parent. You may have had too much responsibility placed on your shoulders at a young age, and you couldn't say no to taking care of your siblings. Growing up with a childhood like that causes a person to believe that the only safe and logical answer is yes because that's all they've ever known. It feels foreign to say no. Saying yes becomes a strategy for coping.

THE IMPORTANCE OF SAYING NO (PROBER, 2019)

Learning to say no is important for many reasons. Constantly saying yes to others will drain our energy emotionally, mentally, and physically. When we learn to say no when it's necessary, we regain the energy we need to address the important issues in our lives. Saying no means saying yes to ourselves. We will be able to keep our own health intact so that we can shine our light more effectively. We will be rejuvenated and full of energy so that when we choose to say yes, we can help others efficiently. Saying no to any situations or people that don't positively serve us will allow us the time we need to heal from any past trauma. This will help us become more balanced and connected—physically, mentally, energetically, and spiritually.

We can't really take care of others if we're not taking care of ourselves, and we can't take care of ourselves if we're always drained from saying yes to others. Saying no can be especially difficult if you are the kind of person who is always making sure everyone else is okay. Your giving and caring nature is a wonderful gift to offer the people in your life. However, to ensure you can continue offering that loving care, you must ensure your needs are met first. Saying no is an essential ingredient for self-care. Setting healthy boundaries will help us have the emotional and physical reserve we need to help others without losing ourselves in the process.

Saying no is imperative because we let other people save themselves and come to their own conclusions instead of us jumping to the rescue every time. If we're constantly helping other people, they will forget that they're capable as well. They will solely depend on us when it would be healthier for them to learn to find their own way. Making mistakes might be what they need in their life to learn and grow.

Saying no is also important because it is a sign of respect, as strange as that sounds. Saying yes to someone when we really don't want to may lead to resentment, negatively impacting our relationship with them. Saying no when that's what we mean indicates respect for ourselves and the other person because we're authentic and honest, which are qualities that cultivate a healthy relationship. Another important reason to say no is because it models this behavior for others in our lives. It sets a positive example of the importance of saying no. By saying no, we might inspire the people in our lives to set their own healthy boundaries with us and others in the future.

Saying no to one thing means simultaneously saying yes to something else. Respectfully declining an event or something that would have taken up our time means we just said yes to using that time for something we'd prefer. This could mean more sleep, going to a yoga class, an evening of movies, or more time with our loved ones.

Saying no means we get to take breaks from changing the world. We get to construct healthy boundaries. We get to relax and take that vacation we've been dreaming of. We get to say no *and* be an HSP.

HOW TO SAY NO AS AN HSP (CHOBY, 2020) (PROBER, 2019)

All of the HSP traits can make it feel impossible to say no. However, with a little bit of boundary setting and some practice, you will be well on your way to saying yes to yourself.

Here are some great ways to build up confidence and authority behind that *no*:

1. Find the level of socialization that feels right for you.

Find a balance that works for you where you're not constantly on the go so much that you exhaust yourself and are not bored from always trying to avoid overstimulating situations. Finding the right level of socialization will make saying no easier. You will be surrounded by close friends who understand your nature and won't get offended when you need a time out. By being in balance, you won't feel so drained and will have time for self-care and self-development.

2. Identify what is important to you and make the decision to protect that time.

Take the time to figure out what makes you happy and what is important to you. It could be as simple as reading or taking your dog for a walk. Once you've got your list of *most important things*, dedicate time to doing what makes you happy every day. Schedule it into your calendar like a meeting if you need to. Your goals and what you value the most don't change, so the more you say yes to other things, the more stressful your life will be. When someone asks you to do something that takes time away from your important list, politely tell them you already have plans and stick to those plans.

3. Make sure people know your limits before possible invitations, so they're not caught off-guard.

If your week is tiring and you're generally exhausted by Friday evening, make it clear to your friends that you need the time off and won't be going out on Friday nights. Making this known and sticking to your guns means they won't even ask you, and you won't feel guilty about saying no. Establish some clear boundaries and let the people in your life know about them. We will be discussing boundaries in more depth in the next chapter.

4. Use humor to say no.

My friend hates swimming. He jokes about it with his next-door neighbors, who love their pool. Because of this, they know he will never accept an invitation to come swimming. They've even stopped inviting him, which is a good thing because they respect his desires. If you don't like dancing and your friends are always asking, decline by making a joke out of it to reduce the tension. That way, you're not directly saying no, but you're still expressing your disinterest in the activity in a lighthearted way.

5. Weigh up your short-term versus long-term regrets.

Ask yourself if you'd rather regret the discomfort of saying no for a few moments or regret the pain and resentment of having said yes for the days, weeks or months it may take to follow through with that commitment.

6. If you haven't already been thinking about it, the answer is no.

When your friend asks you to join their scrapbooking club, meditation group, yoga circle, or after-work happy hour, and your response isn't, "Oh, my gosh! I've been thinking about doing that," that is an indication it's a no or at the very least, "let me think it over." Take the time to think about what you really enjoy doing and what would bring you happiness. If their request isn't something that's going to serve you, it's okay to decline.

7. Delay giving an immediate answer.

Give yourself a moment to consider what you are saying yes to and what you would be sacrificing if you decided to put your time and energy into the request. Take a deep breath before answering and fall back on: "I'll get back to you" or "I need to check my calendar first," so you have time to think about it.

8. Ask yourself how you'd feel if the event or task was tomorrow.

It's easy to think that the answer is yes if the event or task isn't for a few days or weeks because there is a buffer of time making the request seem manageable. Imagine if you had to do the thing tomorrow. Think about how you would feel and let that guide your decision.

9. Know that saying no to the offer doesn't mean saying no to the friendship.

When you say no, be upbeat, positive, and loving so that the person knows it's not them you're rejecting. This can be especially helpful if the person is highly sensitive. Saying no lovingly shows that although you can't fulfill the request, you do care about them as a person. It also helps to keep your pounding heart calm. To keep the friendship alive and healthy, extend your own invitation from time to time.

10. If you're in a season of sacrifice, say no, only for now.

If you are going through a time where it's hard to commit to anything new, express that to the person and leave the door open for connecting at a later stage. An example would be, "I am consumed by design deadlines right now, but when things ease up in a few weeks, let's grab lunch."

11. Don't say maybe when you actually want to say no.

Saying maybe leaves the person with hope for your presence. Saying, "I'll try to make it," prevents the person from planning for the right number of people. A more considerate and kinder answer is a straight no, so no one is left with expectant feelings.

12. Let your devices set the boundaries on your behalf.

Turn off any automatic notifications, so you are not constantly bombarded with social media or email notifications. Use autoresponders on your emails and change your voicemail. Set up the "I'm driving" notification on your phone, so people know you're not available to talk at that moment. It is good to set these sorts of boundaries and say no to people needing you all the time. If you compromise and answer your phone outside of office hours, people will get into the habit of knowing you're always available and won't respect your space.

13. Voice your answer clearly.

When you need to say no, it is possible to be both firm and kind. Avoid overexplaining why you can't or don't want to do what they're asking. Giving reasons for your answer might cause some people to challenge you or find a way to work around your excuse to get you to meet their needs. No is more than enough, so respect your answer without feeling guilty. If you feel like no is too harsh, try saying:

- "Unfortunately, that's just not something I can take on right now."
- "I'm sorry, but that's not going to work for me."
- "That sounds like fun, but I won't be available today."

14. Reflect.

This involves noticing another person's emotions and reflecting them back to them. It might be just what they need and does not necessarily mean you're doing the job for them. For example, if your colleague is constantly asking you for favors, don't give in to doing them but rather say something like, "You seem stressed out today. Is everything okay?" Opening the door for them to vent might uncover the reason they've been using you. Helping them address their emotions will make them feel much more cared for and heard than if you were to just say yes to their requests. If they still need help, having that conversation with them will give you deeper insight into what would really be helpful to them.

15. Be open and honest.

Being open with your friends and family about your need to say no can be very effective. Often as HSPs, we avoid being transparent with others out of fear of rejection or hurting their feelings. However, your friends and family will appreciate it a lot more if you are honest and open with them about your needs and boundaries. That way, they don't have to play the guessing game, and you don't bottle up any resentment toward them.

HOW TO SAY NO WITHOUT FEELING GUILTY (RENZI, 2018)

It might be all good and well to practice saying no, but how do you stop that pang of guilt you feel in your heart? As an HSP, we are so in tune with other people's needs and feelings that it can be difficult to stick to our boundaries and say no without guilt. It can be especially difficult to avoid guilt when it comes to saying no to people who are close to you. At the end of the day, it boils down to putting yourself first and *knowing that you deserve to be put first*. Having a strong sense of what you need and knowing that you can't serve others without serving yourself first is a big part of what softens the guilt. As highly sensitive people, I believe we will always experience some form of guilt when saying no; it's part of who we are. It shows that we care—just as long as the guilt isn't overwhelming and causes us upset or to give in and say yes. Here are some other ways to lessen the guilt when saying no:

1. Tune in.

Take the time to check in with yourself. There might be times when you feel like you need to answer immediately but remember, you are allowed to ask for time to respond. Ask yourself how saying *yes or no* feels in your body. Tune in to your body and notice where in your body you feel the emotion and what your body has to say about it. Is it a negative or positive response? As an HSP, you should always trust your gut. As you practice tuning in and listening to your needs, it will become easier to access your gut feeling and say no without guilt. Being mindful of how your body feels in any given scenario will help you identify old patterns and habits that no longer serve you.

2. Know that it's just not right for you.

Often as HSPs, we feel our answer. Yet, we get stuck in a feeling of guilt if we don't do what others ask of us. In these moments, it is imperative to remember that sacrificing your own needs does not serve anyone. It only makes you less effective at helping them. It might feel like pushing your own needs aside is helping the other person, but you're only harming yourself and the relationship because you're not open and honest. Humans grow through difficult times, so if you're protecting someone else's needs, you could just be preventing them from experiencing an important lesson they need to go through to grow. Remind yourself that if you say yes when you want to say no, you're not actually helping anyone. You will be able to help more people when you take care of yourself first.

3. Rephrase your answer.

Sometimes, you might want to say yes, but with a condition or boundary in place. So, tell the person that, but keep in mind that people respond better to: "Yes, as soon as . . ." than "No, I can't . . ." Saying yes but with a condition in place allows you to give in to your caring and generous nature while still maintaining some healthy boundaries so you have some time for yourself and people don't take advantage of you.

Here are some examples of saying yes while still having your limits in place:

- "Yes, I can help you. This week won't work for me, but I can assist you next week."
- "Sure, I'd like to see you, so I'll come, but I'm just letting you know I'll need to leave early."
- "I can take on the new task, but I will only be able to do so at the end of the month once I've completed my existing deadlines."

4. Express gratitude.

Show yourself some appreciation for those times you manage to stick to your boundaries. If saying no has been a long struggle for you, standing up for yourself can be a profound experience. Show yourself some love and soak up the feeling of empowerment. When falling short and saying yes without wanting to, show yourself compassion. Likewise, expressing gratitude to the people who respect your needs is empowering. It's easy to assume people should act a certain way which can mean taking the people who do honor your boundaries for granted. A simple "Thank you for being so understanding" or "That wasn't easy for me, so I appreciate that you . . ." can go a long way in establishing healthy, intimate relationships. It positively reinforces your relationship dynamic, making the other person more likely to respect your limits again in the future.

For many HSPs, learning to say no without feeling immense guilt can take time. However, it can also be deeply healing. We need to be compassionate and patient with ourselves throughout the process of growing and developing healthier habits.

WRAPPING UP CHAPTER 4

In a world revolving around a work-hard-play-hard mindset, the ultimate act of self-care is to be mindful and fussy about what you choose to commit to. Saying no is a skill that can be built, and the more you practice it, the better you will get. Start small and celebrate every win. Make saying no a challenge for yourself and see how lovingly you can deliver your answer. This will not only preserve your relationships but also honor your own needs. Sometimes as HSPs, we need to get comfortable with the uncomfortable, not pleasing everyone all the time. As Dr. Seuss said, *"Those who mind don't matter, and those who matter don't mind."*

Surrounding yourself with the people who love you for your unique self will make a huge difference. You deserve to live a life of your own design, a life that fills your heart with joy. Living like that is the only way you'll be able to look back and have no regrets.

In the next chapter, we will be covering something that goes hand in hand with saying no: setting boundaries. This chapter will discuss how to create and stick to your boundaries, making saying no a lot easier.

CHAPTER FIVE

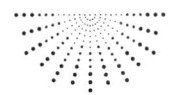

THE BUCK STOPS HERE

The word boundary is defined as anything that marks a border, whether it be a real or imaginary line that indicates the limit or edge. In our personal lives, boundaries are healthy and necessary for our self-care. Without proper boundaries in place, we will end up feeling depleted, taken for granted, taken advantage of, or encroached upon. Boundaries are there to support us in taking care of ourselves. They give us the permission (not that we need it, but they enable us) to say *no* to anything that doesn't positively serve us. Boundaries are there to draw a clear line around what is acceptable and what is not. They are important for creating trust and building healthy relationships. Even if someone doesn't like the fact that you've said no, they will still likely respect you for standing up for what you need and what you believe in.

HSPS AND BOUNDARIES (MACKENZIE-SMITH, 2022)

Setting boundaries used to be extremely difficult for me, and I constantly ended up on the other side of them. I ended up doing things in life I was not passionate about in life—simply to please others. At work, I would accept projects that were pushed onto me even if they weren't mine. In my personal life, I kept quiet in my relationships and never did what I wanted to do until anger and resentment defined me and my actions.

It was only when I finally stopped to do some deep soul-searching work that I realized I felt intruded upon psychologically, mentally, emotionally, and physically. I was always being asked to perform even when I was completely overwhelmed, and the worst part was that I was ultimately the culprit. By never voicing my limits and putting my boundaries in place, I allowed other people to use me while putting my own mental health and success on hold to help them achieve their dreams.

I needed to draw that invisible line in the sand to begin protecting myself, my goals, and my dreams. At first, I felt guilty for letting other people down, and I worried I would offend people. But then I began practicing saying "no" with nothing else behind it—no other excuses or explanations. I taught myself that no was a full sentence, and, in the beginning, it threw a few people off, but I stood strong in my need for boundaries in my life.

Children who are highly sensitive have an acute sense of awareness of the subtle changes in the people around them, particularly with the adults in their life, like parents and teachers. The result is that most highly sensitive children begin adjusting their behavior to make sure others are at ease because they pick up on any little shift in other people's mood, energy, or body language. Although the intention behind this is pure and is part of what makes us as HSPs so special, it leads to us struggling with boundaries because we are so sensitive to the subtle changes in others.

Even though HSPs are exceptionally compassionate regarding the needs of others, we often neglect our own needs. Setting boundaries is difficult for us because, as discussed in the previous chapter, we struggle with the word *no*. We are constantly worried that sticking to our boundaries will hurt other people's feelings or lead to conflict and rejection.

How not setting boundaries manifests in your life (Choby, 2021)

As an HSP, it might feel like you're doing okay. You might have come across the need for boundaries on a blog post or Facebook quiz and have a rough draft of your limits stuffed somewhere in your handbag, but are you actually sticking to them? You might feel like you've got it all under control and saying yes to one more task will be fine, as long as everyone is happy. I've been in your position, and in my observation, here is how *not* sticking to your boundaries creates problems for an HSP and manifests in your life:

1. You are always super responsible.

You take responsibility for tasks that aren't even yours to take on. As an HSP, you feel what other people are feeling and know what they need, and it's ingrained in your nature to want to help them. You may not feel like you can say no, so you say yes. You feel an obligation to help others when they're having a tough time. Guilt drives you to overstep your boundaries because you are worried about what other people think of you.

2. You are afraid to rock the boat in your relationships.

You always show kindness and compassion and give someone the benefit of the doubt if they've had a rough day. You always want your relationships to be on positive terms, so you are always eager to please. Whenever your partner or friends ask you what's wrong, you brush it off and tell them everything is fine, even if you're irritated or resentful. The idea of voicing your opinions or needs leaves you feeling flustered. You are worried that you'll cry because you're angry, or you'll get embarrassed and forget what you were trying to say.

3. You sacrifice your own well-being.

Self-care is the last thing on your list, and that's if it's even made it to the list at all. Saying no and sticking to your boundaries to get some rest doesn't seem like a valid reason. You are afraid you'll be seen as too sensitive or weak if you tell people you're exhausted. Trying to prove you're always capable of being valuable leads to you saying yes to things that aren't good for you. It results in you trying to endure whatever you've taken on even though your health is taking a toll. You've become so accustomed to putting the needs of other people first that you don't actually know what you want or need anymore.

4. People always walk all over you.

You have a hard time holding people accountable for their actions. It's difficult for you to follow through with your friends, family, employees, or even clients when they miss a deadline or don't follow through on something they said they'll do. When someone does something wrong, you fix it instead of confronting them about it, which means they never learn the consequences and don't put in the effort because they know you'll be there to clean up any mess. You let people get away with stuff because you don't want to make them upset or angry, which means you make it known that your feelings are less important than theirs.

Why you need boundaries as an HSP (Martin, 2021)

Everyone needs to have boundaries, but they are especially important for highly sensitive people because we are so strongly affected by other people and our environment. Boundaries are a way for us to filter what we can and can't do. They let in what we can handle and keep out the things that exhaust, overwhelm, or harm us.

In every relationship we have, there is an energy exchange. When we interact with other people, there are two connections at play: the connection to ourselves and our connection with them. Because of our perceptiveness as HSPs, we know what the other person needs, so it feels natural to put them in the spotlight. We may feel the need to keep a positive connection to them, even if it means sacrificing our connection to ourselves and what's important to us. We need to have boundaries as HSPs because if our needs go unacknowledged, we'll end up feeling depleted and resentful. It is possible for two people to share the spotlight.

Without boundaries, it's too quick and easy to say yes without fully considering what the task entails. Having boundaries gives us the buffer we need to have a "tune-in" moment where we make the conscious decision not to take on another person's thoughts, feelings, or energy. Tuning in to ourselves is so important because it gives us a moment to ask ourselves what we need. It can be as simple as making a grocery list of all the stuff you need to get that your family enjoys and then taking a second to include the stuff you like on the list as well.

Boundaries are essentially the limits we need to set to protect ourselves. Boundaries are there to protect us from physical harm, the burn-out that comes with overcommitting, or the discomfort of being around someone with intense or negative energy. Boundaries are there to protect our energetic space. They are a way to strengthen our intuition and better understand how to take care of our needs.

Boundaries you need to set as an HSP (Davenport, 2018)

As HSPs, we cannot let our own fears or what society says dictate who we are. Our lives are in our hands, and we get to choose where we go, who we hang out with, and what we take on. Setting healthy limits will help us stand up for ourselves in all aspects of our lives, and the following are some areas to consider setting boundaries:

1. Living environment.

Our immediate living and work environments are really important. Most HSPs need things to be efficient and organized. Clutter or chaos in our homes or on our desks throws us off course. The good news is that we have a say in how things need to be done. Of course, it's a lot easier if you live alone or work from home, but even then, there are still people to consider. An important boundary to set in your living environment is to let people know how important it is to your well-being to have your things remain orderly. Ask the people involved to either help out or at least respect the rules you have for your space.

2. Crowd management.

It's not always possible to escape a crowd, so it's important to know how to survive when we're in one. Just like a superhero tends to have their suit under their clothes, we need to do the same thing. Except instead of suits, your superpower is your high sensitivity. As an HSP, it is time to own the power you have and not run away from it. You need to stop trying to be normal and embrace who you are. When you're in a crowd, you can stand firm, lean in, and listen to the cries of people in need. However, the trick is to use discernment. You are not responsible for saving everyone, and many people don't want to be saved anyway. They want to feel seen and heard. Choose who you are willing to acknowledge in a crowd, and don't worry about the rest. Your highly sensitive abilities and caring nature might just be the light someone needs on that day.

3. Takers.

There are many takers in this world, and they tend to gravitate toward HSPs because we are natural givers.

We need to set boundaries for when we are around people who only want something from us. It is necessary for our health. If you're in a crowd like in the above point and encounter a taker, it is essential to remember it is not your job to save people and acknowledge you have nothing to give them.

4. Food and beverages.

The saying *"you are what you eat"* is real. As HSPs, our bodies don't only absorb the nutrients or the toxins in the food we eat but absorb the food's energy as well. You may find that some foods have energy that just doesn't agree with your body. We need to create boundaries around food and beverages that don't leave us feeling amazing and not feel pressured into indulging just because everyone else is doing it.

5. Relationships.

This is one place we, as HSPs, definitely need boundaries. We feel the emotions of others as if they were our own, and we don't want the people in our lives to feel pain, so we give ourselves over to every whim of our kids or partners. However, this is not a sustainable way to live. We end up overwhelmed and exhausted and retreat or retaliate in unhealthy ways. We hold on to resentment because we feel our needs are unimportant, but we do this to ourselves. This can create a really uncomfortable duality in our minds. Happy and healthy relationships need clear boundaries. Setting limits starts with knowing your values. When you feel overwhelmed, it is generally because one of your values is compromised. From your values, you can set healing boundaries that will benefit you and the relationships in your life.

6. Television and technology.

Television and technology are both tools used for connection, but they can also negatively affect our health. Watching a movie is a great way to wind down and spend time with your partner, but if the movie is violent, you're probably going to feel really uncomfortable instead of getting a dopamine hit. The same can be said for technology. Our laptops and phones put the world at our fingertips, but if we spend all our time hiding behind them, we're going to miss out on the real connections with the people we seek. Setting boundaries with technology and the TV can be necessary for your health.

7. Time management.

Where attention goes, energy flows. The way we manage our attention will impact how we spend our time. We need to set boundaries around what we focus our attention on throughout the day. Having an if/then protocol in place really helped me manage my attention and time. An example of this might be, "*If* I am tempted to scroll through Instagram while I am writing a blog, *then* I will get up and get a glass of water to drink before sitting back down to work."

Having if/when protocols in place can help us make the necessary choices to stay on track with our intentions.

Examples of boundaries (Martin, 2021)

Here are some examples of boundaries you can set that prioritize your needs:

- Telling your boss that, unfortunately, you won't be able to work late.
- Requesting that someone else change their behavior instead of you being the one to compromise.
- Declining an invitation or request for help from someone.

- Asking a grandparent not to give your kids cookies or candy before dinner time.
- Limiting yourself to one glass of wine.
- Leaving the room when a person makes you uncomfortable or you pick up bad energy.
- Telling your co-worker that you find their jokes or foul language offensive and that you'd like them to stop.
- Hanging up the phone when someone is shouting at you.
- Turning your phone off at a reasonable hour to avoid being woken up by late-night notifications.
- Not answering your phone or email after work hours.
- Creating a meditation practice that you can use to protect your energy.
- Knowing it's acceptable to tell your friends you don't feel like going out for drinks after work.
- Creating the space you need between you and friends or family who you find draining.
- Not answering calls or texts that demand energy when you're feeling exhausted.

HOW TO START SETTING BOUNDARIES (MARTIN, 2021)

People always talk about boundaries as if they are easy to establish, and everyone respects them. However, if you're an HSP who has never really had limits or boundaries, that can be easier said than done. Fortunately, there are ways to learn to set boundaries so you can begin putting yourself first. Learning to set limits doesn't happen in a day, a week, or even a month, but the more you practice, the easier it becomes.

1. Start small.

Don't try to make every change and set too many boundaries all at the same time. Give yourself the time to ease into your boundary-setting goals. Make a list of the boundaries you need to put in place, and start with the smaller ones. As you gain more confidence, you'll be able to move on to the more difficult boundaries.

2. Slow down.

When it comes time to decide what you want to say yes to, you might feel pressured to respond immediately. However, unless it is an emergency, you don't need to respond at that moment. Slow down and take as much time as you need to carefully consider the request or invitation before committing to it. It's completely okay to say, "I need to think about it, and I'll let you know." Taking some time before deciding will help you assess whether the request crosses a boundary, and if it does, you will be less likely to feel guilty when declining.

3. Give yourself permission (Dewsbury, 2020).

Our feelings of guilt, fear, and self-doubt often prevent us from expressing our needs and voicing our opinions. As HSPs, we worry about how other people will react to our requests—this is one of the biggest hurdles we face when setting healthy boundaries. One thing that may greatly help you in many aspects of your life is giving yourself permission to do what you need to do. The truth is that we tend to wait for other people to give us permission or tell us it's okay to speak up about our needs. However, the responsibility to communicate our needs should solely be on us because nobody else truly knows what we need; only we do. So, give yourself permission to set boundaries and limits. Know that you are only responsible for your own actions and are not responsible for the actions of other people.

4. Focus on setting boundaries respectfully and not trying to control how other people respond.

While it's good to consider the feelings and needs of others, it is also important to remember that we can't control how other people react. For example, just because you're polite doesn't mean someone won't yell at you. It is also important to keep in mind that not everything is about you. Often people may lash out at you or seem annoyed when you enforce your boundary, but there's a good chance that something else has contributed to their feelings and actions. Other people's needs are not more important than yours, and it's not selfish to take care of yourself first.

5. Ask yourself some questions.

I find it incredibly useful to journal on the questions below. Seeing the words on paper creates even deeper clarity and makes boundaries easier to set:

- What boundaries do I need to put in place for me to stay in my integrity?
- Am I burdening myself with the energy and problems of other people that aren't mine to carry?

- What would my work environment and personal life look like if I took on less, blamed myself less, and had more respect for my own boundaries?
- What actions, tasks, situations, behaviors, or people am I tolerating that are draining me?

PUTTING YOUR BOUNDARIES INTO PLACE (CHOBY, 2020)

Knowing how to start setting boundaries is the first step, but the next step is to put them into place and start practicing. Sticking to your limits will benefit your overall well-being, mental health, heart, and physical health. When you start saying no to anything that doesn't serve you and yes to what you want to do, you'll find that you will be happier, healthier, and more confident.

1. Know yourself and accept your limits.

Being self-aware will help you make choices that positively serve you. I am a mostly introverted HSP. Although many advantages come with these traits, there are also some limitations. For example, you may know that your job where you spend eight hours in an office with noisy people is draining, so going out after work to socialize is not as fun or relaxing as it might be for other people. You know that you need alone time so you can enforce boundaries that create and protect that time. Everyone will have different limits, but none of us have limitless amounts of time and energy. We need to create boundaries, so we don't overgive, overcommit, and overexert ourselves.

2. Identify what's important to you and decide to protect that time.

It's going to be tricky for you to set boundaries if you aren't sure what your wants and needs are. It is important to identify what feels right and what feels wrong. Begin by compiling a list of what you value and hold close to your heart. Write down how you want to be treated by other people. You can use the list of what's important to you and your values to know when someone is overstepping one of your boundaries. You'll be able to communicate more assertively and clearly because you know what you will tolerate and what not.

3. Pay attention to how you feel and what you need.

Your gut feeling, bodily sensations, thoughts, and emotions are all good indicators of when you need to set boundaries. Tune in to your feelings throughout the day and take the time to evaluate what you need at that moment.

4. Make your limits known.

Make sure the people in your life are aware of your limits before they invite you somewhere or ask you to do something, so they're not surprised when you decline.

5. Pay attention to when you feel influenced by other people (Mackenzie-Smith, 2022).

Generally, people are attracted to the strongest energy in the room and align themselves with that person. As an HSP, it is important to be aware of when this is happening and which person it tends to happen around the most. By noticing this, you will be able to stay true to your authentic, sensitive nature while remaining strong and within your boundaries.

6. Notice where and when you feel the most overwhelmed (Mackenzie-Smith, 2022).

As an HSP, you generally know what affects you the most, but it is essential to check in with yourself often to be aware of what might be going on for you. Pay special attention to the events you attend, the interactions you have, and the responsibilities that leave you feeling overwhelmed and exhausted. Becoming aware of your mental and emotional state is the first step to understanding your own energy. It will help you get clear on any changes you'd like to make or boundaries you need to set to preserve your own personal peace.

7. Me/not-me concept of boundaries (Martin, 2018).

The *"me/not-me"* method helps you define your own energetic and personal space. It helps you declare what isn't yours. Practicing *me/not-me* will help you feel more secure, safe, and strong in almost every scenario. With practice, you will start noticing when other people's thoughts and feelings are affecting you far more quickly, which makes it easier to release with less effort. Here is a simple me/not-me practice to you get you started:

- Stand or sit in a safe, quiet place where you are alone and close your eyes.
- Say your name to yourself. Feel the essence of who you are when you say it. Tune in to the feeling of being your true self.

- Imagine a circle of light around you; it can be any color and can expand two or three feet outward in all directions. This light serves as your energetic boundary. Declare to the universe and yourself that that space is yours and no one else's. Anything that is *not-me* is not allowed in the space and needs to stay outside the boundary circle.
- Say your name again and clear out anything that is *not-me* from your personal space. You can imagine it leaving your circle in any way you wish. I personally like to imagine that anything *not-me* leaves in the form of grey smoke blowing away.
- When you are out in a crowd or around other people, regularly declare your *me/not-me* by performing this practice and visualizing your energetic boundary. Visualize that other people's energies bounce off your space. You can meet their emotions, thoughts, and feelings with understanding and compassion out at the edge of your boundary in your imagination, but their energy isn't allowed entry into your space!

ENFORCING YOUR BOUNDARIES (RENZI, 2018)

There is no point in doing all the work to establish your boundaries if you don't maintain and enforce them. Here are some ways you can build up your boundaries and make them stick (Martin, 2021):

1. Be direct.

Asking for what you want or saying "no" can be intimidating. However, by asking directly and clearly for what you need or desire, you're more likely to be understood and have your needs met. Saying "maybe" or "I'm not sure" when you really want to say "no" will only confuse other people and may lead to them feeling irritated or overwhelmed. When you've put a boundary in place, it is best to express it clearly and directly.

2. Express gratitude.

Show yourself some appreciation for the times you have successfully set and stuck to your boundaries. If you've struggled with this for a long time, standing up for yourself can be profound and empowering. In the times that you fall short, show yourself compassion. It is also empowering to show gratitude to the people that respect your boundaries.

3. Be willing to break the social contract.

To protect and enforce your boundaries, you must be willing to ignore or break the social contract. Simply put, the social contract is the set of unwritten rules that govern our social interactions. For example, getting up and leaving mid-conversation without a word is against the social contract. It can be seen as rude and weird. Another example is walking up to a stranger and putting your hand on them. Generally, people who break the social contract are seen as strange, have low emotional intelligence and are poorly calibrated. However, the social contract is also a way that some people gain influence over others. One of the most obvious ways this is done is through the rule of reciprocation—if someone is seen as doing a favor for you, you should feel a sense of obligation to repay them with a favor. There may be times when it's necessary to ignore or break the social contract to keep your boundaries intact and protect your space.

4. Have consequences in place.

Always choose a consequence you can easily follow through on. Setting boundaries helps to let the other person know what will happen if they don't respect them. Be as specific and realistic as possible. Don't set repercussions that are vague or out of proportion to the boundary being violated. For example, you could say, "Dad, I've told you I don't like it when you comment on my weight. If you continue doing that, I'm going to go home."

5. Be consistent with your boundaries.

If you're inconsistent with your boundaries, you may end up confusing people. If you don't stick to your boundaries, some people will take chances and cross them. Once you set a boundary, do your best to enforce it and always carry out the consequences you've stated.

6. Stand your ground if someone resists.

People might be annoyed or upset with your new boundaries at first. The people in your life may take it personally when you set a boundary with them. They may even intentionally push your boundaries to see what they can get away with. If someone does this, calmly and firmly remind them of your limits and the consequences if they don't respect them.

7. Reassure your loved ones if they are feeling hurt.

Explain that the boundaries you are setting aren't meant to be hurtful or upset them. Setting boundaries with people you care about can be difficult. If your loved one's feelings are hurt, take the time to remind them that you care about them and that your boundaries are there to help your relationships, not damage them.

WRAPPING UP CHAPTER 5

Strong, beneficial boundaries are a keystone for living the life you want, high self-esteem, protecting your health, and maintaining healthy relationships with the people in your life. If your life lacks boundaries, especially as an HSP, it is definitely time to put them in place! The great news is that boundary setting is something you can learn, just like any other skill.

There may be times when it's difficult to stand up for yourself. There may be times when you'll upset people. There may be times when you end up pushing people away because they don't like your boundaries.

However, at the same time, you will be taking charge of your own life and choices. Your boundaries will stop people from making you endure their boundaries.

In the next chapter, we will be talking about how to create your own comfort zone. We will discuss how to protect yourself from outside factors but still be able to live a free and fruitful life.

CHAPTER SIX

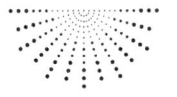

CREATING YOUR OWN COMFORT ZONE

As highly sensitive people, our external environments drastically affect our inner lives. We feel everything so deeply. Our highs are very joyous, and our lows present challenges that affect our ability to cope. Each and every day comes with a sensory overload that can leave us with strong emotions that, if left unchecked, have a negative effect on our mental health and quality of life. That is why, as HSPs, we need to create a comfort zone for ourselves—a sanctuary where we can go to recharge. It is important to develop systems and practices that will help us protect ourselves from outside factors that can be overwhelming.

BECOMING AWARE OF YOUR EMOTIONS (MACEJOVA, 2017)

As an HSP, I find myself struggling with the issue of being rational. The definition of rational is "based on facts or reason and not on emotions or feelings." It is a thought process that employs *objective, logical* and *systematic* methods to reach a conclusion or solve a problem. I don't know about you, but that is not how my brain works. That's not how most highly sensitive people deal with problems. Instead, if there is a problem, we spend a large amount of time wallowing in the feeling the problem evokes. We are prone to holding on to our emotions when trying to find a solution, which clouds our perspective instead of viewing the problem objectively.

There is definitely nothing wrong with that way of processing. However, the danger happens when we lose ourselves in our emotions and don't actually solve the problem. I know that I've been there, blinded with emotion and stuck without an escape. This can lead to a downward spiral of negative thoughts, depression, and anxiety.

It is so important for us to become aware of our emotions and recognize what we're feeling and why those emotions are there. When we aren't conscious of our emotions, it is unlikely we'll figure out how to regulate them. When we become aware of our emotions, they can't control us as much.

You might be wondering, "How is it possible that I'm not aware of my feelings? I am the one who feels everything so deeply after all." Although this is true, we can *feel* something deeply but still not be aware of the fact that we are *feeling* something.

Sometimes our emotions may drive us to do something we didn't want to do (like saying yes or lashing out), and afterward, we feel resentful, shameful, or guilty. This whole situation is complex and can cause a lot of confusion within us. In some cases, our confusion might become so strong that it becomes the problem itself, and that is when rationality needs to kick in.

When you find yourself struggling with negative thoughts that you just can't overcome, take a step back and ask yourself, *what is really happening?* Take a moment to assess the situation and what you're going through. Then ask yourself, how do I *feel* at this moment? Is it fear? Anger? Sadness? If not, what is it? This is another excellent opportunity to grab your journal and free write it out.

Once you can pinpoint exactly what is bothering your mind, you become aware of its presence, and then you have two options: you can *let it be,* or you can do something to *create change.*

Meet your emotions (Rose, 2020)

When strong emotions arise in us HSPs, it can feel like a physical sensation bubbling up inside. Depending on the situation, we juggle handling ourselves with calm compassion or letting our emotions explode. Naturally, the latter can be messy. It is in those moments of explosion that the people around us call us overly sensitive. After all, we let our emotions get the better of us, which is potentially hurtful toward ourselves and others.

This definitely does not mean we need to bottle up our emotions and hope they'll go away on their own. Pushing emotions aside is something that many HSPs do, especially when they've been reprimanded for expressing their feelings.

Instead, we need to implement a simple process that begins with acknowledging that we are feeling something and that *something* has the right to communicate with us. We need to start meeting our emotions, and a good place to start is with this little exercise which is similar to how we meet people.

Start by saying, "My name is (insert your name). What's your name?" Then imagine the emotion replying,

"Hello (your name). I'm sadness mixed with a little rejection." Labeling your emotion as specifically as you can is the first step toward overcoming and releasing it.

Another practice is to simply identify where the emotion is most active in our bodies. Often, shortly after we identify where the emotion is located, its intensity will lessen without us actively doing anything. In this way, our emotions are like puppies who want our attention. The emotions want to be acknowledged. Once we recognize them, they are less likely to rebel and cause us to explode.

Ask yourself some important questions (Macejova, 2017)

Once you are familiar with the emotion you're feeling, you need to ask yourself some important questions. After becoming familiar with the emotion hiding behind your actions, it is essential to analyze it to the best of your ability. The important thing is to be completely honest with yourself when answering them. It will take some time to learn how to be transparent with yourself and others, but it's not impossible. Once again, this is an excellent time to put your pen to paper. Writing things out is an extra form of relief and release when addressing emotions.

- Why do I feel this way?
- What evoked this feeling within me?
- Has this feeling bothered me before?
- Do I have to feel this way? Do I want to?
- Am I focusing on judging myself rather than understanding and empathizing?
- Am I particularly stressed or burnt out right now?
- Did I get enough sleep? Did I eat?
- Am I outside my routine or comfort zone?
- How can I compassionately parent myself right now?

Once you've identified the emotion and what caused it, it can no longer manipulate you into doing something you don't want to do, and it no longer has such power over you.

HAVE A PLAN TO PROTECT YOURSELF

As an HSP, it is necessary to find ways to cope with life's stresses. Most of our stress comes from external stimuli and from being overwhelmed. It is important to have a plan to cope in stressful environments and implement a barrier between us and any overpowering sensory stimuli.

Here are a few ways to protect yourself as an HSP (Radhakrishnan, 2021):

- Add positivity to your life by incorporating activities you enjoy to balance out any additional stress you may encounter. Take the time to do the things that make you happy.
- Avoid any stressors or triggers like violent movies or people who make you feel bad about yourself. Stay clear from any environments where people drain your energy or make heavy demands of you.
- Apply what we covered in Chapter 4, learn to say no to any overwhelming requests, and don't feel bad about it. Create and implement boundaries in your life that make saying no easier.
- Set up a safe space where you can go and recharge. Make your home a safe place with a soothing environment—a sanctuary where you can destress.
- At work, leave a gap between your appointments to allow yourself a chance to decompress. Have set hours when your colleagues can drop by or implement a boundary where you schedule appointments to

avoid random interruptions that spike your stress.
- Implement an 80/20 rule (Bauder, 2021). Always quit while you're ahead in terms of your energy. *I cannot stress this enough.* HSPs often feel tired and feeling burnt out is their normal. Feeling good and maintaining this feeling may be foreign to you at first, but it is normal and necessary. Never let yourself get so overstimulated by one task that it affects your ability to do everything else you need to do. Stop—rest—recharge when you reach 80% stimulation.
- When using social media, set up your accounts to only follow users that post content that positively affect you. Unfollow any accounts that make you feel bad about yourself. Don't aimlessly scroll through your social media feeds. Open the app with a purpose and once you're done, close it again to avoid mindlessly scrolling. Turning off notifications is also wonderfully empowering.
- Stop the glorification of being busy. Society glorifies being busy. We're made to feel that if we're not constantly running around doing things, we're not productive. HSPs need more downtime than other people to recharge. If

you're constantly on the go and continuously stressed and frazzled, you need to reevaluate and slow down.
- Most highly sensitive people love books, so fit in time to read a little bit every day. Reading is the kind of downtime HSPs need that soothes and informs.

DEALING WITH NON-HSPS (ROSE, 2020) (BAUDER, 2021)

1. Accept that non-HSPs won't understand you.

Many people don't understand HSPs, and we're constantly being told to *stop being sensitive* or *just get over it,* even into our adult lives. The fact that people don't feel the way we do or understand why we feel the way we do can leave us feeling like something is wrong with us. We need to accept that other people aren't going to understand us, and it's okay.

2. Collaborate with non-HSPs.

Sometimes collaborating with someone who is non-HSP and extroverted can be a good partnership. Their broad way of viewing the world and the speed at which they make decisions complements an HSPs slower and deeper approach. A partnership between a non-HSP and an HSP will provide different perspectives and energy to the project.

3. Communicate clearly.

Clearly and directly communicating your needs and wants will more than likely come as a great relief to non-HSPs, especially if they're a loved one. As an HSP, it can be difficult to communicate effectively when you're going through an inner storm. But at these times, working through the 'meet your emotion exercise' can be helpful. Once you understand what you're feeling in more detail, it will be easier to communicate with others.

ADVOCATE FOR YOURSELF (SCOTT & GANS)

As an HSP, you may sometimes feel like you've lost control over your life, rights, and responsibilities. Advocating for yourself will help you regain your sense of control and give back the confidence and self-esteem you need to work toward living a happier life.

Here are some ways to advocate for yourself:

1. Educate others.

You don't necessarily need to tell everyone you meet that you're an HSP, but make sure those people important to you know. Clearly communicate your needs and boundaries to your family, friends, and colleagues. Educating other people about how you function as an HSP will help them understand your behaviors and how they can best support you.

2. Believe in yourself.

This is easier said than done but believe in yourself and learn to love the fact that you're highly sensitive. Although being an HSP may have some drawbacks, you can learn to deal with those. However, being an HSP also has many amazing qualities that other people don't have, so celebrate them and accept yourself for who you are.

3. Know your needs.

By knowing your needs, you will be able to put boundaries in place to protect yourself and ensure your needs are met. If you don't know what you need, it will be much easier for people to push you around and take advantage of your giving nature.

4. Have strategies in place.

Make a list of what you'll say to other people in situations where you want to say no and practice it. Know how you'll stick to your boundaries. Have strategies in place that promote your well-being.

5. Communicate and express yourself firmly and clearly.

When you say no, you don't need to give a whole explanation behind your answer. When people push you, practice asserting yourself and standing your ground. If someone tries to reason with you, repeat yourself and reinforce your boundary. It may be challenging initially, but you will find it easier to communicate your needs and stand up for yourself with practice.

CREATE A 'YES LIST'

Creating a *yes list* of activities we know will help calm our nervous system down and doing them at least once a day will go a long way in preserving our sanity as HSPs. My list consists of getting fresh air, taking breaks from technology, yoga, breathwork, meditation and reading. Creating a yes list that you incorporate into your daily routine is a case of *prevention is better than cure.* It's easier to prevent yourself from feeling overwhelmed and burnt out than to manage those emotions once you've been overstimulated. Performing daily activities that nourish you are a lot more effective at preserving your energy than trying to desperately get it back once you're already exhausted.

Here are some ideas for yes list activities (Shuman, 2017):

- Take time every day to recharge and restore yourself with quiet alone time.
- Make art, even if you're terrible at art or haven't picked up a pencil to draw in ages. Do something creative for yourself.
- Make your home your sanctuary to retreat to. If you don't automatically feel relaxed when you walk in the door, assess your environment and take note of anything that causes you to feel distressed.
- Keep your external stimuli to a minimum by avoiding having the radio or TV on in the background as you go about your day (unless you're playing calming music).

- Put your phone in a "do not disturb" mode. Don't answer calls outside of your pre-established hours. Ignore text messages until you are ready to deal with them.
- Embrace minimalism by keeping your schedule, home and wardrobe pared down.
- Implement the *KonMari* method by keeping the items in your home that you really love within sight. Embrace the things that serve you and release the things that don't.
- Fill your house with low-maintenance plants. They will clean the air and make your home feel alive and bright.
- Reduce any clutter and give any important items specific places to live. This will keep clutter from taking over any surfaces. Get rid of junk immediately.
- Keep a few inspiring magazines or books in your bathroom. These will transform using the bathroom into an extra moment for recharging your creativity batteries.
- Invest in one or two Himalayan salt lamps. These lamps provide the same restorative sensation as time spent walking on the beach or by a waterfall. Salt lamps increase oxygen flow to your brain and help cleanse the air around you.

- Take baths, fill them with salts and calming essential oils, and surround yourself with candles and instrumental music. You can settle in with a good book or use it as a time to meditate.
- Give yourself a massage. You can do this after a hot bath or use a heating pad to warm up any areas of your body you're massaging. Use coconut, grapeseed, or avocado oil on your skin. You can even use a fascia tool or a foam roller to break up connective tissue in tight areas of your body.
- Invest in some blends of tea that make you happy and calm, and drink tea regularly. There is nothing a good cup of tea can't fix.
- Eat really good quality dark chocolate. Chocolate is one of the most powerful foods on the planet. It is packed with antioxidants and thousands of aromas and flavor compounds. This makes dark chocolate particularly excellent for HSPs because it is a strong, positive sensory experience.
- Make cooking or baking a fun time for play. Not everyone loves being in the kitchen, but for me, it's a full-body sensory and calming experience. It can be a fun experience to do with a partner or friend as a one-on-one social

activity that explores positive sensory expression and restores peace.
- Open the window, especially after it rains, and let fresh air come into your space. Fresh air works wonders.
- Have lovely scents around your home, office, and car. You could use a diffuser with essential oils, doubling as a humidifier to clean the air.
- Create time for yourself to wind down before bed. Turn off your electronics at least an hour before bedtime and take that hour to journal, do breathwork, read, draw/sketch or meditate.
- In the evening, light a beeswax candle. These candles have a long burn time and smell sweetly of honey. They also cleanse the air.
- Decorate your home with soft natural textures like smooth pottery, cotton or linen pillows and sheets, and natural fiber blankets to create an environment that feels organic. Soft and natural textures are very important if you're very sensitive to touch. You will feel more at ease if the textures you brush up against are soft on your skin.
- Making your bed every morning is so important. The common mindset around making a bed is *why make it when it's going to get messed up again that night?* However, making

your bed every morning makes the bedroom feel so much more peaceful and put together before you get into bed that evening. It also sets a good, productive tone for your day.
- Wash the dishes at night. There is no better feeling than walking into a clean kitchen with no dirty dishes in the morning.
- Burn sage, palo santo, or incense. I burn incense to cleanse my space, freeing me of any negative energy clinging to me or my home. The strong-smelling smoke from these natural incenses provides emotional well-being and clarity.
- Put a morning routine in place, even if it means waking up before everyone else to take in the peacefulness of the new day. Use this time to fill yourself with peace.
- Do a quick yoga routine or light exercise in the morning. It's a great way to really wake up and helps strengthen your spirit to deal with the day.
- Sip hot water with lemon or water with apple cider vinegar in the morning. This is a great way to activate your digestion, especially if you have a sensitive digestive system.
- Make use of breathwork and breathe intentionally. Learn how to do proper deep

breathing and incorporate it throughout your day to reduce any anxiety you may be feeling.
- Spend time in nature or, at the very least, get out for a walk once a week. Walking, especially in nature, helps to calm the mind and spark creativity.
- Massage essential oils on your wrists, temples, and crown. Different essential oils will have different effects on you. You can use mint for headaches and wakefulness or something like lavender when you're stressed out. (Please be sure to dilute accordingly).
- Meditate and simply be with yourself. Meditation is an invaluable resource for getting to know the unconscious patterns of your mind. Meditating will help you become less reactive and more compassionate toward yourself and others.
- Hug your pet. Animals provide a simple, calming, loving connection and don't ask too much of us in return.
- Create a skincare routine to take refuge in. As much as this is about caring for your skin, it's also about creating a routine around going to sleep and waking up.
- Buy yourself a treat or take yourself out on a date. Go for coffee and buy yourself some cute

stationery or spend the day in the botanical gardens and get a print from the gift shop. The options are boundless, but the idea is to go on a date with yourself somewhere that inspires you and treat yourself to a gift that will make you happy.
- Lie down with some crystals. Take some time and place small crystals on areas of your body that need it. You could do this while meditating or doing breathwork.
- Learn to process. You will inevitably become overwhelmed at some point, and no amount of preventative self-care will eliminate the chaotic nature of life. Prayer, meditation, journaling, exercise, creating art, breathing, walking in nature, and therapy are amazing tools for working through negative emotions.
- Bring acceptance and awareness to dis-ease in your body. It is easy to let tension and discomfort overtake your mind but try to actively work on letting it be when you feel uneasy. Become aware of the emotion or feeling and sit with it without judging it. Try to identify the location of that sensation or emotion in your body. See if you can sit with the feeling gently and compassionately until it transforms, shifts, and possibly fades away.

STRESS MANAGEMENT TIPS AND TECHNIQUES (SCOTT) (VERGHESE)

HSPs are more vulnerable to stress because we feel everything so deeply. Something that may not stress out a non-HSP could cause a lot of anxiety for us. It is important to practice some stress management tips and techniques to maintain a healthy well-being.

1. Learn to detach when needed.

Often you may find yourself attached to pleasing people, a desired outcome, a particular person or situation, your job, or constantly being busy. However, when that attachment has a negative impact on your health and well-being, even if it's temporary, it is important to learn to detach so you don't end up overwhelmed and burnt out.

2. Learn to meet with your emotions.

Get in the habit of asking yourself how you're feeling throughout the day and acknowledge any negative emotions. By noticing their presence, you'll be able to gain better control over how they cause you to react.

3. Seek the help of a professional.

Seeking the guidance of a counselor, psychologist, spiritual healer, or even speaking to someone close to you can help you deal with any anxiety or stress. Sometimes simply voicing your emotions can help you process and work through them.

4. Avoid any triggers.

If you know a certain situation or person triggers you, avoid it as much as possible. If you don't have to be out in a large crowd, rather stick to hanging out where you're comfortable and with whom you're comfortable.

5. Take time out when you need it.

If you're at a social gathering and you begin to feel overwhelmed or stressed, take some time to gather yourself and process any information.

6. Clear your energy often.

Ground yourself and clear the energy around you and your home often. HSPs often pick up the energy and emotions of others that don't belong to you, and you need to clear it away.

7. Form healthy lifestyle habits.

Exercise regularly and implement a good sleeping routine. Do your best to eat as healthy as possible and drink enough water.

8. Be your authentic self.

Don't try and hide your sensitivity. Embrace it and voice it to the people who are important to you. Being open and honest about what makes you unhappy will help the people in your life understand when you need a break or time to yourself. Being your authentic self will attract the right people into your life.

WRAPPING UP CHAPTER 6

Creating our own comfort zone is an important part of being an HSP, and there are many ways to do it. It is vital to have an external environment that is nourishing and calming. As HSPs, we need to fill our days with the activities on our yes lists to prevent feeling overwhelmed and overstimulated. However, we cannot always control life, so it is also essential to learn to create a peaceful internal environment. This starts with acknowledging and recognizing our emotions so we can process them and ultimately release them. Once we have a handle on our feelings, we can better handle the situations we are faced with.

In the next chapter, we will talk about embracing who you are as a highly sensitive person. Society constantly makes us feel like something is wrong with us, and we need to change, but in the following chapter, we will cover how to harness your HSP qualities and use them to create the best possible life.

CHAPTER SEVEN

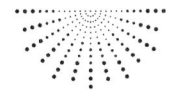

EMBRACE YOUR HIGHLY SENSITIVE SELF

As an HSP, I constantly felt the need to want to "cure" myself. I felt like I was living with a disadvantage and just wanted to be as normal as the people around me. It took me a while to embrace the fact that being highly sensitive is *who I am*. Once we as HSPs know how to manage our unique characteristics, we get to turn what we see as flaws into strengths. Life becomes less challenging, and we are able to use our sensitivity to our advantage. Once we learn to embrace who we innately are and overcome the challenges we as HSPs face, like saying no or people-pleasing, we can use our incredible gifts to help the world (on our terms, of course).

THE STRENGTHS OF AN HSP (CHLOE, 2019)

The process of accepting our sensitive selves and discovering our strengths can be a challenging journey. As HSPs, we have to fight all of the negative messages telling us we're "less than." We have to fight the messages that might feel true as we struggle to keep up with non-HSPs in this fast, loud, and overstimulating world. Often, we may feel left behind, lonely, different, or out of place. However, as we begin to prioritize our needs and value ourselves, our internal dialogue shifts to one of self-acceptance. Here are some of the most powerful strengths of a highly sensitive person (Wilding, 2021):

1. We are sensitive.

First of all, one of the best things about being an HSP is being sensitive (as the name suggests). While it can seem like a double-edged sword at times due to how overwhelming it can be to feel so much and so deeply, sensitivity is a gift. It makes us thoughtful and compassionate. We care more about people and treat them with care. This is why HSPs are some of the gentlest and kindest people you have ever met.

2. We are self-aware.

The definition of intrapersonal intelligence is an awareness of one's emotions, beliefs, motivations, and goals, and HSPs certainly have that down. As HSPs, we are deep thinkers by nature. We gain a greater insight into ourselves because we are so in touch with our own thoughts and feelings. We are attentive and introspective, meaning we rarely ever feel unsure of how we feel or what we think about something. Thus, we can always trust ourselves and our gut feeling to make the right choice.

3. We have a lot of empathy.

Empathy and sensitivity go hand in hand, so it should come as no surprise that most HSPs are amazing empaths too. Being an HSP allows us to feel what other people are feeling and to put ourselves in their shoes. Because we are already so in tune with our own feelings, we are better able to perceive the feelings of others as well. This makes it easier for us to relate to those around us and understand their different points of view.

4. We are intuitive.

The HSP nervous system is constantly absorbing tons of information. This means that we often "just know" things in ways that are difficult to explain. When making decisions, this intuition adds a deeper layer that gives us clarity and discernment. We are able to tap into ourselves and access our gut feeling.

5. We are good listeners.

Another great quality that many HSPs have is that we are excellent listeners. Our natural intuition makes us more empathetic and observant than most, allowing us to quickly understand the subtleties of a person's gestures, voice, body language, etc. This makes us more attentive and receptive to others, making us great best friends, partners, and sources of emotional support.

6. We are good mediators.

Highly sensitive people are fantastic mediators because of our great resolution skills. As HSPs, we always try to maintain positive and harmonious relationships with others, and confrontational situations make us uncomfortable. Because we are such empathetic listeners, we can often fill the gap between two conflicting parties.

7. We work well in teams.

Our unique ability to pay attention to the smaller details, take other people's feelings into account and weigh up different aspects of multifaceted decisions make us extremely valuable in a team environment. We are well suited to offering analysis and input rather than deciding whether or not to push the red button.

8. We are able to have deep and meaningful conversations.

Small talk can set off our "this feels meaningless" siren, and we'll typically have a hard time ignoring this feeling once it's switched on. As HSPs, we feel more comfortable talking about deeper and more meaningful topics than chit-chat about movies or plans for the weekend. HSPs are great as a "go-to" friend or colleague when someone needs to have a chat about something important.

9. We are creative.

It is believed that creativity is closely associated with being an HSP. This is probably because most highly sensitive people are visionaries with a rich inner world of their own. Since we experience both negative and positive emotions on such a deep level, this kind of intensity lends itself well to our creative self-expression. This can be expressed through writing, painting, designing, photography, filmmaking, and other creative skills. Even if you can't paint or draw, you likely have a good appreciation of art.

10. We have great manners and are likable.

Our heightened awareness of other people's emotions makes us highly conscientious. We always pay close attention to how our behavior affects others and have the good manners to show for it. Our kind, caring, empathetic and sympathetic nature makes us extremely likable to other people.

11. We have a deep passion.

To the uneducated non-HSP, our emotional sensitivity can make it seem like we are constantly overreacting. Others may dismiss us as nothing more than wishy-washy daydreamers or romantics, but in truth, there is so much more to us than that. Being an HSP means we seek to live life wholeheartedly and authentically. This vulnerability is what fuels us with the passion for pouring our heart and soul into everything we do.

12. We value integrity.

Most of us highly sensitive people are guided by our values, morals, and principles. We have a strong sense of what is right and wrong, and we believe in ideals of morality and equality. As HSPs, we generally feel uncomfortable with anything that's overly violent, aggressive, or demeaning, so we can't stand injustice. We value integrity and pride ourselves in our character, which is an admirable trait.

13. We are adaptable.

HSPs can easily read the room and adapt to whatever environment they find themselves in. By picking up on the subtle energy omitted from the people around us, we are able to adapt and be whatever is needed at the moment—whether that be a friend, a meditator, a caregiver, or simply just be there.

14. We are resilient.

As HSPs, we are deeply affected by everything from news headlines, someone in pain, or an injured animal to heartbreaking news about a close friend. Trying to keep our hearts open is a constant battle because it would be so much easier, less painful, and less exhausting to close ourselves off from the world. However, when we get knocked down, we keep getting back up. We are not weak; we are warriors!

15. We live life to the fullest.

We do not live out our days half asleep. Being highly sensitive means being present and living in each and every moment. Our sensitivity makes us careful not to overstimulate ourselves and be overloaded with thoughts, emotions, and sensations. Doing this allows us to take things at our own pace, and in turn, we remind those around us that it's okay to slow down every now and then and just enjoy everything life has to offer us.

16. We have a willingness to improve and change.

Although we might overreact to the initial criticism, we also tend to contemplate and explore things deeply. And this exploration of criticism plays out well for us in the long run. Our inability to "shrug it off" helps us make the necessary and appropriate changes.

17. We are one of a kind.

Last but most definitely not least, being an HSP means that we are special. There will probably be some people out there who can't understand what it's like to be like us and see the world through our eyes, but we need to know that our uniqueness is not our weakness. Being highly sensitive is a gift granted only to a few rare people, which is part of what makes us extraordinary.

FIVE WAYS TO ACCESS YOUR STRENGTHS (SNOW, 2018)

To access the amazing strengths we as highly sensitive people possess, we need to live a lifestyle that is aligned with our needs and wants and supports our personality. Here are five pointers to help you start accessing your strengths:

1. Making space for downtime.

The most essential practice for you as a highly sensitive person is getting enough quiet downtime every day. This downtime also includes getting enough quality sleep to feel rested. It is so common for HSPs to feel overwhelmed because we absorb and notice everything around us, whether that be consciously or not. Then our brains process and reflect on all of that information very deeply. The more we multitask and overschedule, the more depleted we become and the more sleep we need. It's like running a laptop until it overheats. That is essentially what is happening to your brain and nervous system when you take on too much.

Tip: Try giving yourself one hour of uninterrupted quiet time before bed each night, as well as a midday break going for a walk outdoors or sitting quietly.

2. Prioritizing our needs.

With enough downtime, you'll be able to set boundaries and place limits on your commitments to other people. At the end of the day, no one knows how tired you are except for you. Saying no is a difficult task for HSPs because we feel guilty as though we're disappointing others. However, prioritizing your needs is absolutely essential to avoid exhaustion.

Tip: Set a limit on how many social invites you agree to attend each week, and make sure to set one day per week aside as a self-care day. It is also beneficial to say "yes" on your terms and practice saying "no" out loud to yourself or others when it feels necessary.

3. Taking time for self-reflection.

Since you feel everything so deeply, it is imperative for you to take time to reflect and sort through your emotions on a regular basis through self-reflection.

Tip: Generally, self-reflection involves journaling; however, creating art, engaging in expressive movement, or talking with a friend can all be effective forms of introspection. Find a practice that feels in alignment with your needs.

4. Just breathing.

When you feel overwhelmed and anxious, it is often because your nervous system has gone into *fight-or-flight* mode. You may notice that your breath is shallow, you have difficulty concentrating, or you physically tense your muscles when this happens. To calm your nervous system down, breathe mindfully and slowly.

Tip: With your eyes closed, take a deep breath in through your nostrils and then breathe slowly out your mouth through pursed lips. Do this at least three times, taking slow, deep breaths. See if you can make each exhale slightly longer than the previous one.

5. Be kind to yourself.

More often than not, you internalize the negative messages you receive about being highly sensitive. This makes it difficult to accept and be gentle with yourself during a moment of struggle. However, being critical of yourself will only keep you trapped. Instead, use self-compassion practices to calm your inner critic and soothe any negative thoughts about yourself.

Tip: Whenever you are being critical of yourself, take a moment to pause, close your eyes, and place your hand over your heart. With your soft inner voice, say, "My emotions make sense. May I be compassionate to myself and accept myself as I am. The way I am feeling is only temporary."

When we create a lifestyle that aligns with our needs, our strengths can truly shine through, and we can live our best lives.

THE VALUE YOU ADD TO RELATIONSHIPS AS AN HSP (GOOD THERAPY, 2015)

HSPs make great partners and friends. We add a lot of value to the relationships in our lives because of our highly sensitive traits. Once we understand and embrace our sensitivity and are able to communicate our needs to our partners and friends clearly, these relationships can be amazing. Here are some ways that you, as an HSP, add value to your relationships:

- You are naturally compassionate and aware of your friend or partner's emotions and feelings. This means you are great at being supportive and loving when they need it. You care deeply about their well-being and always want the best for them.
- Your observant nature notices the subtle goodness and beauty in other people. The result of this is that you point out your friend or partner's inner beauty, draw out their gifts, and are a great source of affirmation and confidence-building for them.
- Your profound self-awareness combined with the understanding of what drives others emotionally helps to create powerful, lasting relationships.
- You are blessed with the amazing gift of perspective, and you see both sides of the coin. Your strong empathy makes you better equipped to see the other person's point of view. You are naturally more relationship-oriented than agenda-oriented, making you a great mediator or peacemaker. This perspective gives you strength and

perseverance to work through challenges when they arise.
- You easily notice nonverbal cues and pick up subtle nuances that others may not see, so you can often address someone's needs even if they don't vocalize them. You are very caring, empathetic, and emotionally responsive to the needs of others.
- You are a grounding, calming presence when you are centered and healthy. This is one of the greatest strengths of an HSP. You radiate calm energy to your loved ones, which nourishes them.
- Your high levels of depth, empathy and emotional intelligence make you an excellent partner or friend for those who can relate to and understand your emotional nature.
- You are deeply perceptive and can support your friend or partner to better understand themselves and your relationship. Highly sensitive people are meaning-driven. You are dedicated and willing to work hard to create a deeply meaningful connection in a relationship. This makes you more likely to have a rich, healthy and committed relationship despite any challenges you may face.

- You are probably the go-to person for relationship advice because of your deep insight into other people's emotions.
- You have strong intuition and are excellent at knowing when people are being dishonest or insincere, helping you sniff out anyone who is fake or full of it.

HOW TO HARNESS YOUR HSP QUALITIES FOR YOUR OWN GOOD

Think of your sensitivity as a superpower, and other people will too. Owning your sensitive nature is the best way to encourage others to appreciate it as well. When you stop apologizing for your nervous system's reaction and start seeing it as a rare gift, your mindset around your sensitivity will change entirely for the better.

Here are some ways to harness your sensitivity and make it work for you (Wilding, 2016) (Hoshaw, 2021):

1. Realize that you are not alone.

Around twenty percent of the population is highly sensitive. You do not have a disorder but rather a distinctive gift. Find comfort in knowing others like you also have similar feelings and challenges.

2. Reframe your emotions as strengths.

Take time to reflect on your emotions and reframe them. Once you start digging into your emotions, you may find you have a lot of anger. Some of that anger may be toward yourself and what you view as flaws, and some of it may be toward ideologies, culture, and society for making you feel like you need to fix yourself. Reframe your emotions in a way that can help you. For example, don't let your anger toward the world make you shut down your sensitivity. Rather, see the "feeling" part of yourself as one of your greatest strengths and use it to show love and compassion to those who need it.

3. Start telling the people who matter.

Start telling the close people in your life that you are highly sensitive. Share your HSP-ness with them so they can better understand you. In most cases, the information will be well received. Not everyone will understand, but the people who truly care about you will make an effort.

4. Regularly practice self-care.

Practice self-care and center yourself often. Use your "yes list" from Chapter 6 and schedule those activities that calm and ground you into your day. Keep this list nearby and whenever you feel overwhelmed, choose something that will make you happy and do it.

5. Have confidence in your communication skills.

Most HSPs display rare strengths in key areas of emotional intelligence, also known as emotional quotient (EQ). This is the ability to recognize and understand emotions in yourself and others. Your sensitivity is a gift for communication that can help your workplace run smoothly and your career and life flourish. HSPs communicate effectively because not only do they hear the words coming out of other people's mouths, but they are also in tune with subtle gestures and tones.

6. Use your creativity to solve problems.

As a creative person, you are deeply in tune with your inner world. This can lead to fascinating discoveries, innovative solutions to problems, and a unique sense of clarity that most of your peers don't get to experience.

7. Prepare for stimulating scenarios.

As much as possible, try to anticipate questions and think about your answers ahead of time, keeping in mind that overpreparation can also be a crutch. Consider creating an outline with the "highlights" you want to cover the most. Make sure you don't rely on winging it; if you're feeling flustered, you'll forget what you wanted to say.

8. Flip the "don't be so sensitive" motto on its head.

A call to be more sensitive by connecting with our own feelings and those of others may be just what we need. In an era with depression on the rise, reframing sensitivity and care as a strength can be a saving act, which is desperately needed in this world.

9. Know that being an HSP is a gift.

Earlier in the chapter, we spoke about all of the strengths and the value you add to other people's lives. Embrace all the good that comes with your innate traits and let go of the idea that you have to *fix yourself*. Being highly sensitive is a quality that not everyone has, and it's something the world needs.

WRAPPING UP CHAPTER 7

Next time somebody tells you to toughen up or criticizes you for being too sensitive, remember all the amazing strengths and qualities tied to your sensitivity and that the world needs more HSPs. Instead of being hard on yourself for being too sensitive, focus on cultivating your creativity, compassion, intuition, and empathy because those are incredible assets—you can use them to do amazing things for yourself and other people.

The next chapter is a bonus chapter written for your friends, family, and colleagues. It will help them become aware of your sensitivities and how to be more considerate of your needs.

HELPING FELLOW HSPS

Even though we make up twenty percent of the population, being an HSP can feel pretty lonely and isolating. For a number of years, I simply determined that I was at a deficit in life. After I started educating myself on how to thrive as an HSP, I began helping others find their power, joy and health. This brings me such a feeling of fulfillment and purpose, and I want the same for you!

You have the same ability to help other HSPs like yourself by taking a moment and leaving a review on Amazon. As a self-published author, this is the most helpful and effective way to reach and help more people. If you found this book helpful, please leave a review via the link/QR code below. Your willingness to share can positively impact someone's journey forever. Your words have the capacity to help someone feel heard, validated and empowered. Huge love and blessings to you.

https://geni.us/AmazonReviewLinkLove.

BONUS CHAPTER

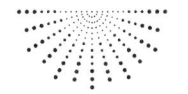

HOW TO DEAL WITH THE HSP IN YOUR LIFE

The term HSP is still relatively new, and because high sensitivity only affects one in every five people, it's easy to see why some non-HSPs have no idea how to deal with or understand an HSP. You can show this chapter to the people you interact with on a regular basis who will benefit from knowing about high sensitivity. This will make it easier for them to know how they can help you manage your sensitivities and how to be more considerate of your needs.

HOW TO IDENTIFY A HIGHLY SENSITIVE PERSON (MIND TOOLS CONTENT TEAM)

The most notable characteristic of high sensitivity is depth of processing. This means that HSPs absorb more information from their surroundings than others and analyze it more deeply—often unconsciously.

Here are some ways to identify an HSP:

- They are calm and non-confrontational by nature. They often have a comforting energy, and people gravitate toward them.
- HSPs are conscientious, creative, hardworking, and dedicated, but too much sensory or social stimulation can overwhelm them and make them stressed and withdrawn.
- They demonstrate awareness, empathy, action planning, an advanced level of cognitive processing, and responsiveness to other people's needs.
- HSPs are aware of their surroundings and particularly sensitive to stimuli that affect their senses. For example, HSPs can be overwhelmed when their surroundings are too loud, bright, or cold, and they can be stressed out by large groups of people, lots of chatter, chaos, and clutter.

- They can't handle violence, cruelty, torture, or injustice of any kind. They will opt for a light-hearted movie over a horror.
- HSPs generally won't have a breakdown at work as they tend to deal with stress in private, spending their free time on their own to recharge their batteries.
- They need time by themselves to get back to a place where they no longer feel overwhelmed. HSPs will feel the need to retreat to a calm, quiet space after being around people.
- HSPs are natural caregivers and often overcommit because they have difficulty saying no and feel the need to please people.

HOW TO SUPPORT HIGHLY SENSITIVE PEOPLE (MIND TOOLS CONTENT TEAM)

HSPs come with many unique traits that are often difficult to understand. However, these characteristics are what make them unique, and there are certain things you can do to make their lives easier and support them.

1. Accept them.

Don't try to help them *overcome* their sensitivity. Sensitivity is not an ailment that needs to be cured.

They aren't able to change their triggers. Instead, make sure you're open, receptive, and understanding and work hard to create and sustain a positive and relaxed environment for them. Let them know that you appreciate their traits and accept them for who they are.

2. Address sources of stress.

Ask them what overwhelms or irritates them and try not to trigger their sensitivities rather than dismissing them as unimportant or not legitimate.

3. Let them work or be alone.

Since HSPs are highly aware of their environment, they tend to feel uncomfortable and perform poorly when you observe them working, micromanage them, or put them on the spot. They may also need to spend time alone to distance themselves from any stimuli that may be affecting them.

4. Provide a quiet place for them if possible.

If you work with them, provide a calm working environment wherever possible. If you live with them, allow them the private space they need and can retreat to when things get overwhelming.

5. Give advanced warning.

Many HSPs manage overstimulation by preparing or developing routines, plans, and strategies for upcoming events. While you can't always prevent sudden schedule changes, try to give your highly sensitive team member or loved one as much notice as possible before meetings, events, gatherings, or activities. If they become flustered when last-minute changes occur, give them time to recover their composure.

6. Encourage them to take action.

If they feel overwhelmed or stressed, you could suggest that they spend a few minutes alone and take some deep breaths. You might also encourage them to take solo walks during their breaks and listen to soothing music with earphones. If they learn to become aware of what overwhelms them, they can avoid those triggers or take breaks afterward to get back on track.

7. Advocate for them.

When you hear someone criticizing them or sensitivity in general, stand up for them and explain that it's an innate trait and there is nothing wrong with them.

Encourage others to rethink the misconceptions and stereotyping around high sensitivity.

HOW TO COMMUNICATE WITH HIGHLY SENSITIVE PEOPLE

HSPs are neurologically different from others and have many gifts, but their intense reactions to people and situations often cause confusion, conflict, and heightened emotional turmoil. To foster positive and constructive relationships with an HSP, the non-HSP should use special communication strategies.

Here are some ways to communicate with an HSP (Cveal, 2019):

1. Pause for processing.

HSPs deeply process internal and external information, and the resulting stress can be overwhelming. It will appear that they have difficulty expressing themselves. Be aware of silence and avoid interrupting them or giving them the words you think they are looking for. When they have finished speaking, tell them how you understood what they said.

2. Notice and gently suggest alternative behaviors.

How you point out weaknesses and flaws can make or break relationships. Avoid a condescending, patronizing, overpowering, or parental tone of voice. Instead, say, "I noticed that . . ." or "Did you know that . . ." or "Another approach might be to . . ." These words carry a lot less shame and blame.

3. Timing.

Choose the right time to give your feedback. If you or they are tired, in a hurry, or upset, your feedback will likely be less appreciated. *No one* likes to hear they've done twenty-five things wrong at the same time—that will be especially traumatizing for an HSP. Pick the top one or two to tackle in one session. Engage in a discussion about problem-solving that prevents emotions from escalating. Notice when they are overwhelmed and take a break. HSPs may need more time to process a mistake and formulate a solution than you.

4. Praise and encourage authentically.

Be honest and modest in your praise. Many HSPs cringe when they receive a compliment, even a well-deserved one. To reduce stress for both of you, try not to get too excited about their successes or lack of progress. If your emotions are not kept in check, your highly sensitive friend will lose face if they disappoint you.

5. Invite questions.

Positive speaking and a supportive attitude will make it easier for an HSP to ask questions. If you seem unapproachable, they will be reluctant to bother you when they're facing a problem. You may be the safe place they are looking for.

6. Don't rescue.

Do not save them from distress unless it is absolutely necessary. HSPs learn from their mistakes but with more pain than non-HSPs. If you come to their rescue too often, they might never gain the thick skin needed to survive life. Your constant rescuing could hinder their growth.

WHY YOU NEED HSPS IN YOUR LIFE

HSPs have an insightfulness making them aware of people's potential problems before they become serious, and they have the perception to know how to deal with them. They can effectively interpret and resolve interpersonal problems and help create harmonious working environments. HSPs tend to be hardworking, careful, and vigilant about quality, making them great to work with. They can see the details and the big picture and visualize different possibilities. Highly sensitive people are often creative, perceptive, excellent communicators, and very gifted. They love deeply and are natural-born caregivers. HSPs are very empathic and compassionate. They appreciate the small things in life and will encourage you to live in the moment.

CONCLUSION

"Highly sensitive people are too often perceived as weaklings or damaged goods. To feel intensely is not a symptom of weakness, it is a trademark of the truly alive and compassionate. It is not the empath who is broken, it is society that has become dysfunctional and emotionally disabled. There is no shame in expressing your authentic feelings. Those who are at times described as being a "hot mess" or have "too many issues" are the very fabric of what keeps the dream alive for a more caring, humane world. Never be ashamed to let your tears shine a light in this world."

— ANTHON ST. MAARTEN

Being highly sensitive means you're probably going to cry when the dog dies at the end of a movie. It means you can't handle hordes of people and need scheduled time to retreat to be alone. It means you are always piling way too much onto your plate because you don't want to say no, and as a result, you're so exhausted that you just want to run away. It means you are constantly picking up on subtleties around you, making you feel like you always need to please others.

Being highly sensitive also means you are a beautiful soul filled with much compassion and empathy for others. It means you appreciate nature and beauty on a whole new level. It means you have high levels of self-awareness and relate to past and present events with insight, meaning, and understanding, which assists you in piecing the jigsaw of life together. It also means you appreciate all that life has to offer and use your creativity and intuition to nurture others and bring value to this world.

Being an HSP comes with its perks and challenges but learning to manage these means you don't have to watch life from the sidelines. One of the challenges you need to overcome as an HSP is learning to say no to protect your energy. Saying no is difficult because you may be afraid of conflict and don't want to disappoint people. You are afraid of rejection, and if you always say yes, the chance of being rejected decreases.

However, saying yes to others means saying no to yourself. Always running to meet the needs of others and agreeing to anything anyone asks you to do will only leave you feeling exhausted and eventually resentful. At the end of the day, you need to come to terms with the fact that you won't always be able to please everyone—no matter how hard you try. To live a healthy and fulfilled life, you need to start putting your own needs first. You must learn to take care of yourself first and foremost because, when you stop taking care of yourself and fall out of balance, your ability to help others will be affected.

The inability to say no and being a people-pleaser is dangerous for you as an HSP because both have the opposite outcome of what was intended. Constantly attending to other people's needs makes you feel like you'll get a positive reaction from them. However, a lot of the time, it ends up making people feel weary of you. I know that sounds incredibly harsh, but people will feel subtly uneasy around you, whether it's conscious or unconscious. When you enter people-pleasing mode, you are hiding your true self because you suddenly appear not to have any needs or wants, and people can pick up that it's not authentic. They may withdraw from you, which causes a painful cycle of rejection to occur.

The good news is that it is completely possible to stop saying yes to everything and stop people-pleasing. One of the best ways to stop yourself from taking everything on is to take a moment before you answer. Don't answer immediately—stall for time if you have to. Another important aspect of breaking free from people-pleasing is saying no with conviction and learning to sit with the discomfort. Don't answer with "maybe" or "I don't know." Be strong in your "no." The uncomfortable feeling won't last, and learning to sit with it will take away its power. Once the power is diminished, nothing can guilt you into saying yes.

Another essential step in learning to say no and quitting your people-pleasing tendencies is to set proper boundaries. Knowing your limits and being willing to communicate those boundaries with the people in your life is essential. If you have solid boundaries in place and feel like people are asking too much of you, it will be easier to say no and reinforce what you can and can't do because you have something to stand behind.

The best way to begin setting boundaries to protect your energy and well-being is to start small and get clear. Don't set all your boundaries in one day; you'll end up feeling overwhelmed. Start slowly and enforce one boundary at a time. Make a list of the things that make you happy, the things you want to do every day, and find a way to protect that time.

Focus on setting respectful boundaries for yourself, and don't worry that your boundaries will cause a reaction in other people. You cannot control how everyone responds. If you create boundaries with other people's feelings in mind, they won't be strong, and people may end up taking advantage of you. You need to create solid limitations and focus on enforcing them so other people know where they stand and what line they cannot cross.

When it comes to enforcing your boundaries, you need to be direct and communicate with the people in your life. Stand your ground and have consequences in place so people know they cannot get away with expecting you to help with everything. It might take some time for everyone to adjust but be persistent and consistent. If anyone's feelings happen to get hurt, reassure them that it's not personal.

It's time to accept your highly sensitive self and your unique gifts. I know that being an HSP can be difficult but following the advice in this book will set you free. Trying to be someone you are not will be more exhausting and a lot more effort than embracing who you are and working to overcome any challenges you face.

There is so much to love about yourself and your sensitivity. The world needs you to embrace yourself and shine your light. So go boldly, go courageously, and go sensitively!

REFERENCES

Acevedo, B. P., Aron, E. N., Aron, A., Sangster, M.-D., Collins, N., & Brown, L. L. (2014, July 4). *The highly sensitive brain: An fmri study of sensory processing sensitivity and response to others' emotions.* National Library of Medicine. Retrieved January 17, 2022, from https://www.ncbi.nlm.nih.gov/pmc/articles/PMC4086365/

Aron, E. (n.d.). *Are highly sensitive people more creative and intelligent than other people?* The Highly Sensitive Person. Retrieved January 17, 2022, from https://hsperson.com/faq/are-hsps-more-creative-and-intelligent/

Aron, E. (n.d.). *The highly sensitive person.* The Highly Sensitive Person. Retrieved January 16, 2022, from https://hsperson.com/

Aron, E. (n.d.). *The highly sensitive person.* The Highly Sensitive Person. Retrieved March 15, 2022, from https://hsperson.com/

Bauder, P. (2021, March 24). *Emma-Louise parkes: How to survive and thrive as a highly sensitive person.* Medium. Retrieved November 16, 2022, from https://medium.com/authority-magazine/emma-louise-parkes-how-to-survive-and-thrive-as-a-highly-sensitive-person-4b68a4d04f8a

Bradberry, T. (2016, August 30). *9 signs you're a highly sensitive person.* Forbes. Retrieved January 15, 2022, from https://www.forbes.com/sites/travisbradberry/2016/08/30/9-signs-youre-a-highly-sensitive-person/?sh=1cc823f362e3

Cerbo, K. D. (2016, June 23). *How highly sensitive people can break free from people pleasing.* IntrovertDear.com. Retrieved November 16, 2022, from https://introvertdear.com/news/highly-sensitive-people-these-tricks-can-help-you-break-free-from-people-pleasing/

Cherry, K. (2021, April 28). *What is willpower?* Verywell Mind. Retrieved November 17, 2022, from https://www.verywellmind.com/willpower-101-the-psychology-of-self-control-2795041

Cherry, K. (n.d.). *How to stop being a people-pleaser.* Verywell Mind. Retrieved November 16, 2022, from https://www.verywellmind.com/how-to-stop-being-a-people-pleaser-5184412

Chloe. (2019, October 5). *10 strengths of a highly sensitive person.* Psych2Go. Retrieved January 17, 2022, from https://psych2go.net/10-strengths-of-a-highly-sensitive-person-2/

Choby, M. (2020, May 21). *10 simple ways to say no so you'll be less overwhelmed by your calendar.* Be So You. Retrieved January 16, 2022, from https://besoyou.com/blog/ways-to-say-no/

Choby, M. (2021, March 3). *Setting new boundaries in your relationships? this will help you actually do it.* Be So You. Retrieved January 16, 2022, from https://besoyou.com/blog/set-boundaries-relationships/

Cole, C. (2021, May 3). *How toxic generational patterns affect hsps (and what you can do to break them).* Highly Sensitive Refuge. Retrieved February 16, 2022, from https://highlysensitiverefuge.com/how-toxic-generational-patterns-affect-hsps-and-what-you-can-do-to-break-them/

Crosthwaite, A. M. (2020, April 27). *I'm a highly sensitive person. here's what I wish more people knew about hsps.* mindbodygreen. Retrieved February 15, 2022, from https://www.mindbodygreen.com/articles/i-am-a-highly-sensitive-person-heres-what-i-wish-more-people-knew-about-hsps

Cveal. (2019, February 27). *6 ways to communicate with highly sensitive people.* Mindful Communication. Retrieved November 17, 2022, from https://www.mindfulcommunication.com/6-ways-to-communicate-with-highly-sensitive-people/

Daniels, E. (2021, April 7). *4 things most people don't know about being a highly sensitive person.* Dr. Elayne Daniels. Retrieved January 16, 2022, from https://www.drelaynedaniels.com/4-things-most-people-dont-know-about-being-a-highly-sensitive-person/#:

Davenport, C. (2018, July 10). *The 7 most supportive boundaries for sensitive people.* Medium. Retrieved November 16, 2022, from https://colettedavenport.medium.com/the-7-most-supportive-boundaries-for-sensitive-people-56b1632299e4

REFERENCES | 191

Dewsbury, V. (2020, December 28). *How to set boundaries when you're a highly sensitive person.* Thought Catalog. Retrieved January 16, 2022, from https://thoughtcatalog.com/vanessa-dewsbury/2020/12/how-to-set-boundaries-when-youre-a-highly-sensitive-person/

Fraga, J. (2019, April 19). *Being "highly sensitive" is a real trait. here's what it feels Like.* Healthline. Retrieved November 16, 2022, from https://www.healthline.com/health/mental-health/what-its-like-highly-sensitive-person-hsp#1.-Being-an-HSP-affected-my-childhood

Good Therapy. (2015, November 12). *8 ways highly sensitive people make the world a better place.* GoodTherapy. Retrieved January 17, 2022, from https://www.goodtherapy.org/blog/8-ways-highly-sensitive-people-make-the-world-a-better-place-1112157

Granneman, J. (2014, August 20). *Highly sensitive people and the problem of people-pleasing - introvert, dear.* IntrovertDear.com. Retrieved January 16, 2022, from https://introvertdear.com/news/people-pleaser

Granneman, J. (2015, July 8). *Are you highly sensitive? {take the highly sensitive person test}.* IntrovertDear.com. Retrieved January 15, 2022, from https://introvertdear.com/news/highly-sensitive-person-test-quiz/

Harwin, C. (n.d.). *Highly sensitive people/introverts: Are you a people pleaser?* The Highly Sensitive Person Publishing Company. Retrieved January 16, 2022, from https://www.thehighlysensitiveperson.com/highly-sensitive-people-introverts-are-you-a-people-pleaser/

Hoshaw, C. (2021, January 20). *Why your sensitivity is really a strength.* Healthline. Retrieved January 17, 2022, from https://www.healthline.com/health/mental-health/why-your-sensitivity-is-really-a-strength#Be-more-sensitive

Kaufman, A. (2022, March 30). *4 key boundaries to set as an HSP - and how to maintain them.* Highly Sensitive Refuge. Retrieved April 16, 2022, from https://highlysensitiverefuge.com/4-key-boundaries-to-make-as-an-hsp-and-how-to-maintain-them/

Macejova, S. (2017, September 25). *Why it's important for hsps to become more aware of their emotions.* IntrovertDear.com. Retrieved

November 16, 2022, from https://introvertdear.com/news/emotions-hsps-aware/

Mackenzie-Smith, K. (2022, January 29). *How to actually set better boundaries - the HSP way*. Highly Sensitive Refuge. Retrieved February 16, 2022, from https://highlysensitiverefuge.com/how-to-actually-set-better-boundaries-as-an-hsp/

Martin, S. (2018, January 12). *How to set energetic boundaries and stay true to yourself*. Psych Central. Retrieved January 16, 2022, from https://psychcentral.com/blog/imperfect/2018/01/how-to-set-energetic-boundaries-and-stay-true-to-yourself#Applying-theMe/Not-Me-concept-of-boundaries

Martin, S. (2021, August 5). *Boundaries for the highly sensitive person*. Live Well with Sharon Martin. Retrieved January 16, 2022, from https://www.livewellwithsharonmartin.com/boundaries-highly-sensitive-person/

Mathews, A. (2015, February 17). *Why is it so hard to stop people pleasing?* Psychology Today. Retrieved November 16, 2022, from https://www.psychologytoday.com/za/blog/traversing-the-inner-terrain/201502/why-is-it-so-hard-stop-people-pleasing

McNamee, D. (2014, June 23). *'sensitive people' show heightened activity in empathy-related brain regions*. Medical News Today. Retrieved March 15, 2022, from https://www.medicalnewstoday.com/articles/278589

Mind Tools Content Team. (n.d.). *Managing Highly Sensitive People*. MindTools. Retrieved January 17, 2022, from https://www.mindtools.com/ag510h5/managing-highly-sensitive-people

Mueller, K. (2017, November 20). *5 misconceptions about highly sensitive people that need to go away*. IntrovertDear.com. Retrieved January 16, 2022, from https://introvertdear.com/news/highly-sensitive-people-hsp-misconceptions/

Orloff, J. (2019, January 11). *The difference between highly sensitive people and empaths*. Psychological and Educational Consulting. Retrieved January 15, 2022, from https://www.psychedconsult.com/the-difference-between-highly-sensitive-people-and-empaths/

Prober, P. (2019, March 20). *The sensitive person's guide to saying no*.

Highly Sensitive Refuge. Retrieved January 16, 2022, from https://highlysensitiverefuge.com/sensitive-person-guide-say-no/

Radhakrishnan, R. (2021, March 17). *What is the meaning of being sensitive?* MedicineNet. Retrieved February 15, 2022, from https://www.medicinenet.com/what_is_the_meaning_of_being_sensitive/article.htm

Radhakrishnan, R. (2021, March 17). *What is the meaning of being sensitive?* MedicineNet. Retrieved January 16, 2022, from https://www.medicinenet.com/what_is_the_meaning_of_being_sensitive/article.htm

Rakshit, D. (2020, October 28). *Why some people are more sensitive than others.* The Swaddle. Retrieved January 16, 2021, from https://theswaddle.com/why-some-people-are-more-sensitive-than-others/

Renzi, M. N. (2018, October 12). *How to say no without guilt as a highly sensitive person.* Melissa Noel Renzi. Retrieved January 16, 2022, from https://melissanoelrenzi.com/say-no-without-guilt/

Rose, C. (2020, January 29). *4 ways to tap into your strengths as an HSP.* Highly Sensitive Refuge. Retrieved January 16, 2022, from https://highlysensitiverefuge.com/ways-to-tap-into-your-strengths-as-an-hsp/

Sagansky, G. (2021, July 2). *Are you a highly sensitive person? here's how to tell.* Vogue. Retrieved January 15, 2022, from https://www.vogue.com/article/are-you-a-highly-sensitive-person-heres-how-to-tell

Sapala, L. (2018, August 20). *Highly sensitive people, you're not responsible for other people's feelings.* Highly Sensitive Refuge. Retrieved February 16, 2022, from https://highlysensitiverefuge.com/highly-sensitive-people-not-responsible-for-other-peoples-feelings/

Scott, E. (n.d.). *How to cope with stress when you're highly sensitive.* Verywell Mind. Retrieved January 16, 2022, from https://www.verywellmind.com/ways-to-cope-with-stress-when-highly-sensitive-4126398

Scott, E. (n.d.). *What is a highly sensitive person (HSP)?* Verywell Mind. Retrieved February 15, 2022, from https://www.verywellmind.

com/highly-sensitive-persons-traits-that-create-more-stress-4126393

Shuman, R. (2017, April 18). *43 self-care practices for the highly sensitive person*. Will Frolic for Food. Retrieved January 16, 2022, from https://www.willfrolicforfood.com/blog/2017/04/43-self-care-practices-for-the-highly-sensitive-person.html

Snow, A. (2018, October 24). *5 ways to access your strengths as a highly sensitive person*. Highly Sensitive Refuge. Retrieved January 17, 2022, from https://highlysensitiverefuge.com/highly-sensitive-person-access-strengths/

Snow, A. (n.d.). *Highly sensitive person trait + characteristics*. Expansive Heart Psychotherapy. Retrieved February 15, 2022, from https://www.expansiveheart.com/highly-sensitive-person

Sólo, A. (2018, October 29). *5 misconceptions every highly sensitive person has to deal with*. Highly Sensitive Refuge. Retrieved January 16, 2022, from https://highlysensitiverefuge.com/highly-sensitive-person-misconceptions/

Sólo, A. (2020, June 17). *The difference between introverts, empaths, and highly sensitive people*. Highly Sensitive Refuge. Retrieved November 16, 2022, from https://highlysensitiverefuge.com/empaths-highly-sensitive-people-introverts/#:

Trittin, L. (2018, August 6). *How highly sensitive people can stop saying yes when they want to say no*. Highly Sensitive Refuge. Retrieved November 16, 2022, from https://highlysensitiverefuge.com/highly-sensitive-people-say-no/

Verghese, S. G. (n.d.). *6 effective tips to manage stress when you are a highly sensitive person (HSP)*. Sports news. Retrieved November 16, 2022, from https://www.sportskeeda.com/health-and-fitness/6-effective-tips-to-manage-stress-when-you-are-a-highly-sensitive-person-hsp

Weiss, S. (2018, July 18). *7 myths to stop believing about highly sensitive people*. Bustle. Retrieved November 16, 2022, from https://www.bustle.com/p/7-myths-to-stop-believing-about-highly-sensitive-people-9752736

Wilding, M. (2016, November 1). *Your sensitivity is a career superpower.*

here's how to use it. Forbes. Retrieved January 17, 2022, from https://www.forbes.com/sites/melodywilding/2016/11/01/5-ways-to-turn-your-sensitivity-into-strength-at-work/?sh=2bb60c17518e

Wilding, M. (2021, March 26). *12 reasons why high sensitivity is your greatest strength in the Workplace.* Better Humans. Retrieved January 17, 2022, from https://betterhumans.pub/12-reasons-why-high-sensitivity-is-your-greatest-strength-in-the-workplace-dff2853155a9

Wright, S. (2020, November 20). *Am I highly sensitive, and empath, or just shy?* Perspectives Holistic Therapy. Retrieved May 15, 2022, from https://www.perspectivesholistictherapy.com/blog-posts/2020/11/20/am-i-a-highly-sensitive-person-empath

Printed in Great Britain
by Amazon